Lord Roll was born in Austria and came to England in 1925. He served in the Ministry of Food, the Treasury, in Whitehall, Washington and Paris. He was involved in the Marshall Plan, NATO and the first Brussels negotiations, ending up as Permanent Under-Secretary of State in the Department of Economic Affairs. Since 1966 he has been active in the City as an investment banker and is now Senior Adviser to Warburg Dillon Read.

Where Are We Going?
The Next Twenty Years

ERIC ROLL

faber and faber

First published in 2000
by Faber and Faber Limited
3 Queen Square London WC1N 3AU

Phototypeset by Intype London Ltd
Printed in England by Clays Ltd, St Ives Plc.

A CIP record for this book
is available from the British Library

ISBN 0-571-20262-4

2 4 6 8 10 9 7 5 3 1

To Jo and Liz

A Grateful Father

Contents

Preface

A few years ago I wrote a book called *Where Did We Go Wrong?*
Ever since then I have felt a sort of moral obligation to write a
sequel that would attempt to show how errors might be avoided,
or at least mitigated, in future. The occasion for the re-examin-
ation both of the facts and of the problems, as well as of my own
views, is given by the change that occurred in our political situation on 1 May 1997. On that day, after eighteen years of
Conservative government, first under Mrs Thatcher and later
under Mr Major, a Labour government again took office. Not
only was this an important and indeed virtually secular change,
but the fact that Labour came into power with an unprecedented
majority and the main opposition party was reduced to a very
minor role, not to say to temporary political impotence, provides
a landmark change that deserves a new look at the future.

Furthermore, the advent of a Labour government with the
present majority not only guarantees a smooth parliamentary
passage – certainly for one parliament – for whatever legislation
it wishes to enact, but also provides considerable probability of at
least one other parliament after this one. In other words, it gives
it ten years of power, and since the Conservatives were in power
in the post-war period first for twelve and later for eighteen years,
makes it not unlikely that Labour may remain in power even after
the first ten years.

I have chosen twenty years as my period of reference – in
other words, a period during at least half of which the present
government, with such changes of personnel as will inevitably
occur, will be running our affairs.

The assumptions that I have made are strengthened by the
extraordinary fact that even after eighteen months in power, which
is when I started writing this book, the popularity of the Labour

government and of its leader, Prime Minister Tony Blair, is not only undiminished, but perhaps even stronger than it was before. Two party conferences have now taken place since Labour came into power and although there are inevitably signs of differences of opinion among the party faithful, to which I shall refer later, nevertheless his mastery over his own followers and to a very large extent over the country is still undisputed and indeed, one might say, almost unprecedented.

I have kept what follows as short as I have been able to and inevitably therefore there has had to be a considerable, and sometimes very radical, selection both of themes to be dealt with and of amounts of space and argument devoted to those that are. I hope nevertheless to have provided a broad picture relating primarily to the economic, and to some extent the social, aspects of government as well as to purely political ones. I also hope that I have dealt with those adequately, although I have inevitably had to leave out extremely important themes (such as criminal justice) that require highly specialized treatment. Some passing references, however, have been made to certain problems and possible treatment of these problems by the government as well as to what I might call spontaneous social and economic evolution during the period under review that will illuminate some of the more thoroughly dealt with aspects.

The book falls into three parts:

1 Where we were
2 Where we are
3 Where are we going?

I have, however, had to depart from this division in relation to the special topic of Europe.

Eric Roll
March 1999

PART ONE

Where We Were

The Conservative Years

The end of the century, the start of a new millennium, would provide an obvious point from which to look ahead: to consider where our country should be going in the next two decades and to speculate on where it is likely to go. The next year is likely to produce and set in train developments that will profoundly affect the world environment in which our own country's destiny will be played out. Looking at our immediate environment, the European Union (which has now taken the critical decision on Economic and Monetary Union, which we have not joined) will in the next months decide on many of the important terms under which the Single Currency will be operating and on a detailed *modus operandi* for the European Central Bank.

Looking further afield within Europe, in the next two years the process of preparing and eventually admitting to membership a number of Central and Eastern European countries will make further progress, and the process may indeed have started by the end of those two years.

The great country of Russia is already undergoing very considerable changes. It is by no means certain in what direction the market reforms that have been initiated since the fall of the Soviet regime will continue, what kind of balance will be struck between an authoritarian regime, possible remnants of a command economy that are still favoured by many within Russia and the growth of the market. What the future will be of the less attractive features that accompany the growth of capitalism (as indeed they did the early days of capitalism in our own and other Western European countries), and how they will gradually give way to a fundamentally law-based society, is still very uncertain. Within the next two years much in this direction may become clearer.

Across the Atlantic the United States will be preparing for a

3

new election in which the two terms of a Democratic presidency will be put to the test and may be replaced by a new Republican presidency. If so, and if, as is likely, there continues to be a Republican Congress, that will be a relatively new situation for the USA and for the world.

In the Pacific area, Japan will no doubt continue to suffer from turbulence in the financial sectors and it is not excluded that recent bankruptcies of brokerages and banks will continue. The whole future of the dynamics of the Japanese economy may well be reformed and changed in the next two years from an essentially export-based economy, with all the consequences for the currency and for the monetary system, towards greater reliance on domestic demand and investment in infrastructure in areas in which it is badly needed. Japan will be affected, as it has already been, by what is happening in other countries in Asia, and in South-East Asia particularly. The next year or so will certainly show whether the massive rescue operations by the International Monetary Fund and various individual countries for South Korea and other countries have been effective, or whether more support will be needed, or whether what support has already been given will be, so to speak, frittered away in financial speculation in the stock markets without any fundamental reform of what has brought about the present turbulence. The same is true of other important countries in South-East Asia that have shown considerable weaknesses in their financial structure that present menaces to the stability of the whole system in countries such as Malaysia and Indonesia in particular. China, the growing giant in the East, set to become within a decade or so one of the leading economies of the world, has so far withstood successfully the consequences of the Asian financial turmoil. The extraordinary combination of the political and social structure, largely still that of the past, with the gradual abandonment of the command economy and the growth of more liberal economic structures in finance and industry, has so far worked out reasonably well. It remains to be seen whether the pressure that will undoubtedly grow for liberalizing the political and administrative system will be successfully accommodated.

4

Certainly from an economic point of view the prospects for China, particularly with the incorporation of Hong Kong, are more benign than for many other countries in the area.

All these factors, which will, as I have said, change the environment within which our own country will be proceeding over the next twenty years, are not, however, the main reason for taking a look at the future. In May 1997 a new government came into power in Britain. After eighteen years of government by the Conservative Party, Labour is now in government. This is a very substantial change not only because it comes after the longest period this century of government by one political party, but also because the party now in power purports to be different, indeed fundamentally changed, from the Labour Party as it has been known for a hundred years. This in itself provides a very important reason for speculation about the future. It is a reasonable assumption that the party now in office will remain so for one decade at any rate, i.e. for two parliaments – half of the period that we are now considering for the future.

Was 1 May 1997 the great watershed in the destiny of the British people? The rhetoric that followed the victory of the Labour Party that day, with an unprecedented majority and after eighteen years out of office, would suggest that it was. That kind of rhetoric is, however, not unknown in the history of British politics this century. 1918 was supposed to usher in the construction of a country 'fit for heroes'; 1945, after another dreadful war, was supposed to produce the 'new Jerusalem' in this green and pleasant land, with an important welfare safety net and secure employment for all. 1964 was supposed to 'get Britain going again' by applying the 'white heat of modern technology', also after a long period (twelve years) of government by the other party. 1979 was supposed to put an end to all that 'unprincipled' mishmash of policy that had gone before under governments of different political colours. It was to give free rein to enterprise; it was to 'take government off the back of British business'; it was supposed to 'roll back the frontiers of the state' and release all the energies of a free society.

5

This is not the place to rehearse in detail what happened to all these great expectations and large promises. It is worthwhile, however, before examining the prospects of the 1997 promise being realized, to look briefly at the last two decades while Labour was in the wilderness and the country was governed by a Conservative majority for twelve years under one prime minister and for six under another.

At first glance the repetition of these high promises – and I have only mentioned a few – and the inevitable shortfall in performance might well encourage a rather cynical approach. '*Plus ça change, plus c'est la même chose*' might appear to be an appropriate description. In fact, this would be an extreme view. Of course, in the past these promises have certainly not been realized to the extent expected. But things have changed and continue to change; and, although tremendous blemishes remain, of which more later, there have been improvements. Even in the last twenty years there have been some, although many of the flaws and defects of our society have grown worse during that period.

The last two or three years of Labour government in the late seventies, presided over by Jim Callaghan, saw the culmination of the declining grip that the party had on affairs and on the electorate. It was Jim Callaghan's bad luck that this happened under his premiership, and particularly that it took the form of great difficulty with the unions in accommodating their action and their demands to the macro-economic environment, amounting almost to a split in the traditional relationships between the unions and the party. The environment had deteriorated considerably as a result of the crisis of 1976, which was brought to an end by the imposition (virtually on the instruction of the International Monetary Fund) of much stricter fiscal and monetary policies, which worsened the economic situation and increased unemployment. The attempts to bring the unions into a co-operative role in coping with this situation, mainly through wage restraint, the long-standing difficulty of applying an incomes policy, which had plagued Labour governments right from the beginning of the Wilson administration, grew worse and finally led Jim Callaghan to call an election in 1979. It is at this point that the eighteen years of Conservative government began.

The actions of the Conservative government over the next eighteen years, and more particularly during the first twelve or so when Margaret Thatcher was in charge, were very controversial and remain so from the point of view of a historical assessment of what actually happened. Opinion is sharply divided on whether this was a period of unrelieved deterioration socially, politically and economically, or whether indeed it was the beginning – in the minds of some people unfortunately brought to a premature end – of a real change in the economic style of government and the political climate of the country. My own opinion is that there were a few developments that produced some improvement on previous policies, which were to a large extent an inevitable reaction to what had gone wrong before and also a consequence of what was happening in the rest of the world. The net effect – the net balance – of that period, and perhaps more particularly of the first twelve years of that period, is, I believe, very negative. Politicians, particularly prime ministers at the outset of their government, are not necessarily on oath (to paraphrase Dr Johnson) when they make their first statement, usually on the steps of 10 Downing Street, as in Margaret Thatcher's case. The references to St Francis and to the all-embracing benevolent attitude of the new government towards the population as a whole were soon contradicted by its actions. Many people who are critical of what happened under the Thatcher administrations will nevertheless give her credit for having coped with the problem of the trade unions, a problem that had become virtually intractable at the end of the Labour government. There is some truth in this. The situation in the latter days of the Labour government had become difficult and was aggravated by the attitude of the media – most of them by no means well disposed towards Labour in any case. Many, particularly sections of the press, had made the most of what had come to be known as the 'ungovernability' of Britain. There is no doubt that the unions had lost a good deal of that public sympathy that the British people are generally ready to bestow on them. Going back to the Heath administration, the effect of strikes, including the accumulation of garbage in the streets of London and other cities, the chaos in the administration of the Health Service, had certainly made much of the population, if not hostile, at any rate extremely sceptical about the role played by the trade unions. This was exploited to the full by the Thatcher government, and the actions of preceding Labour governments, particularly in the early days of the Wilson administration with the government's 'beer and sandwiches' evenings with trade unions at 10 Downing Street, were described as the beginning of a 'corporate state'. This was of course nonsense, but it carried enough plausibility to make it possible for the Conservative government, without losing popular support, to enforce considerable legislative and practical restrictions on future union power. These extended to sympathetic strikes and the introduction of compulsory ballots.

The battle against what was thought of as the trade unions' overweening power was particularly fierce with the Miners' Union, led by a very militant faction under Arthur Scargill. In dealing with it, the government was helped by the long-term declining tendency of the mining industry, which has continued to this day.

More generally, the new Conservative government certainly cannot be said to have been successful. The National Health Service was exposed to various experiments, introducing market pressures, self-funding, independent budgets and so on, the net result of which, when looked at some twenty years later, was to create an enormous bureaucracy with a very substantial proportion of the total state expenditure on health falling under the administrative rubric rather than on services to patients themselves. The periodic outbreaks of discontent among doctors, and particularly among the nursing profession, did not come to an end and indeed were rather aggravated as a result of these various reforms.

In education too the various attempts to introduce new forms of funding, particularly in higher education, had mixed results. They did not produce the sophisticated and highly efficient system that was aimed at. In the secondary and primary levels of education a good deal of chaos remained, and many of the defects, particularly of large classes, inadequate training of teachers, periodic outbreaks of non-cooperation on the part of the teaching profession, continued and indeed were rather aggravated. Uncertainty about curricula added to the confusion.

The last five or six years of Tory government under a new Prime Minister, John Major, showed signs of a desire to return to some of the more easy-going, shall we say, or more comfortable forms of earlier Conservative government; but the legacy and influence of Thatcher, in whose government Major had served as Chancellor of the Exchequer, remained overwhelming and was shown very much in continued difficulties on many of the fronts that Thatcher had already experienced.

Without a doubt, much the most lasting and deep-seated defect of the whole period of Tory administration, only slightly ameliorated under Major, was the government's attitude to Europe. Here again there was a contrast between strident, extreme rhetoric and actual practice. Despite the plain hostility towards the general philosophy of the European integration movement to be seen right through the eighteen years of Tory government, there was a good deal of practical co-operation in many of the advances made by the European Community, later the European Union. The most important of these was the creation of the Single Market. Britain co-operated fully both in its establishment and in the implementation of its various steps. We were, for some time at least, far ahead of all our partners in the Union in adopting the various directives designed to make the Single Market a reality. The processes of the Union were greatly helped by the adoption of the Single Act, which Mrs Thatcher subsequently claimed to have agreed to with great reluctance and only after a good deal of persuasion from her cabinet colleagues. She was later said to regret greatly that she had given way on this score. At any rate, despite these various battles, particularly on the budget, marked by very strident language in the negotiations, a good deal of practical participation continued. It should incidentally be noted that the apparently tougher attitude gained a certain amount of popular support. This is a feature of the reaction of the British people to the conduct of its representatives in foreign negotiations that has occurred again and again, although it serves mainly to make one feel good rather than to achieve the best results.

One major development in the European Community in which Britain did not take part, or fully take part, was the institution of the European Monetary System in 1979, about the time the Thatcher government came into power. This was the result of action by Helmut Schmidt, then Chancellor of Germany, Giscard d'Estaing, President of France, and Roy Jenkins, President of the European Commission.

The European Monetary System was an elaborate and complex system designed to keep fluctuations in the exchange rates of the various currencies of the member countries within bounds. The most important operating part of the system was the European Exchange Rate Mechanism, which fixed limits expressed as percentages within which these fluctuations were to be kept. It put an obligation on the member countries to keep the currencies within those limits; and together with this obligation went a parallel obligation on their monetary authorities to support each other in this process. Britain, although a member of the European Monetary System, did not participate in the European Exchange Rate Mechanism – the ERM – from the beginning. She did eventually join it in 1992, just about the time when Major, then Chancellor, was about to succeed Margaret Thatcher as Prime Minister. The belated entry of Britain into the European Exchange Rate Mechanism was itself a drawback, because the processes of support and policy moves designed to fulfil the obligations of the mechanism had been going on for a long time without Britain being active within it, though co-operating to some extent. Moreover – and this was the most important factor – when we joined the Exchange Rate Mechanism, we did so at the rate of DM2.95 to the pound, which was generally regarded at that time as excessively high and which, by all accounts and rumours that have emerged since, was the direct result of an instruction by the then Prime Minister, i.e. Margaret Thatcher. The overvaluation of the pound had an immediate negative effect on our export trade and indeed very seriously damaged our prospects of growth and employment, which, as always, depended to a considerable degree on the buoyancy of our exports. The overstrong pound produced the usual balance of payments consequences and created considerable difficulties. These culminated in the crisis, only a very short time after we had entered the Exchange Rate Mechanism, when we had to abandon it. Italy followed suit, the lira also having been overvalued; and the whole mechanism was virtually suspended. In theory it remained in being, but with the permissible exchange rate margins raised from $2^1/_4$ per cent each side of the middle value to 15 per cent. This, of course, made it more or less a theoretical rather than a practical operating device.

The general situation of the government at that time was sufficiently weak to make many people expect that the election of that year would bring about a Labour victory. This in fact did not happen: to everybody's surprise the Conservatives won again, this time under the new leader, John Major, Margaret Thatcher having been jettisoned before the election. There is very little doubt that the change of leadership had something to do with the unexpected victory of the Tories; and, again quite unprecedentedly in modern times, it led to a further five years of Conservative government.

As I have already said, the general climate of that period was rather different from what it had been. This was partly due to the relief brought to our economy by departure from the Exchange Rate Mechanism, which immediately resulted in a considerable decline in the value of sterling vis-à-vis both the D-Mark and the dollar and with it a considerable improvement in our export trade, in economic growth generally and in employment. The Major government benefited a great deal politically from this economic upturn and was able to stay in office for its full term.

It was also during this period that the Gulf War, in which Britain took a prominent part, helped, as often happens, to boost the popularity of the government and in particular that of the Prime Minister. Nevertheless, as the time of the parliament was beginning to draw to a close, various signs of what might be described as something similar to metal fatigue began to appear. There were increasing differences between ministers, very rarely overt, but they found their way into the rumour mill. The media began to report dissensions within the Cabinet between some of the hawks of the earlier Thatcherite time as against the more liberal and progressive elements (though, given the approach of the election, personal rivalries were probably more important). At that time too the problems of monetary policy were beginning to be a matter of speculation and dissension. The Chancellor Kenneth Clarke, who had shown in many respects a rather different and more progressive attitude to affairs in regard to Europe as well as the economy, had instituted a series of periodic meetings with the Governor of the Bank of England. These were made public through the issue of minutes, with a time lag of course, but nevertheless indicating the trend of their discussions and attitudes. It became clear that while the fiscal stance of the government remained pretty much unchanged, Mr Clarke was on the whole inclined towards a more liberal policy in regard to monetary restraint.

Taking it all together, Kenneth Clarke's influence on the affairs of the government, especially his much more forthcoming attitude towards European integration and even towards the Economic and Monetary Union proposal, did make a difference. In general, therefore, the attitude of the Major administration was less antagonistic than that which had prevailed under Mrs Thatcher. One of the great difficulties one imagines Mr Major as Prime Minister had to contend with was that he took over a government that had already been in power, that had relied on the same political majority in parliament for twelve years and had been run by an extremely aggressively minded leader. In these circumstances striking out on his own was not easy. He did attempt to change the general atmosphere, which had been left behind in a very divided state. There is no doubt that one of the worst legacies of the Thatcher administration was precisely the general climate of opinion that had been created. The stridency, the divisive rhetoric, the widely quoted distinction between those who were 'one of us' and those who were not, the also widely quoted distinction between the 'wets' and the 'dries' certainly were not conducive to creating an atmosphere of consensus in which difficult measures could be passed without creating a feeling of exclusion among substantial proportions of the people concerned. The atmosphere under Major was slightly better, but many of the greater attempts that he made to redirect political debate into more constructive channels were not successful. Certainly he also suffered from one of the great hazards of politics, namely the very risky use of slogans, which only rarely come off and more often than not boomerang. This was, for example, the case with the famous 'back to basics'. It is a curious thing that politicians are so prone to go all out for slogans, not remembering that more often than not their effect is the opposite of what is intended. One formidable example that should deter others was Harold Wilson's 'the pound in your pocket has not been devalued'.

While the gradual decline in popularity of the Major government, substantially promoted by various personal scandals involving some ministers and the general accusation of 'sleaze' in governmental affairs, was proceeding and had certainly created an expectation of a possible Labour victory in the election in 1997, the size of the Conservative defeat was quite unexpected. It is an old saying in British politics that oppositions do not win elections; governments lose them. In this case, while it was certainly true, the size of the majority does suggest that there was also a positive swing to Labour and not merely a reaction against the existing government; and this may well have been due to a general sense of dissatisfaction with the current state of the economy. Despite apparent improvements – though variable – particularly in profits in the corporate sector, and the decline in unemployment, there was a widespread feeling that nothing much had been done to create a more progressively secure economic and social environment. Moreover, the differences between the rich and the poor had grown more obvious, with serious impoverishment at one end and extraordinarily high – not to say obscene – executive remunerations at the other end. This may have added to the electorate's mood when they went to the polls on 1 May 1997.

Europe, although widely debated and more or less definitely an object of hostility on the Tory side, did not seem to play a major part in the electorate's decision when they voted. At any rate it can be said that, quite apart from the huge majority that the Labour Party achieved in the election of 1997, its arrival in power was greeted with a surprisingly widespread welcome. The media, which are in the vast majority not even neutral but on the whole anti-Labour, showed a considerable restraint, and in some instances even welcome, towards the new government. It is true that the leadership of the party had to some extent prepared for this by showing itself – and emphasizing that it wished to show itself – to be 'business-friendly', and had established connections with a number of leading businessmen and business firms before the election took place, thus contributing to the feeling that this new government was unlikely to be basically hostile to business, that the old idea that profit was a dirty word was certainly no longer in force. Somewhat paradoxically perhaps, the fact that the whole of the top leadership had virtually no experience in government before, combined with its relative youth, worked in its favour rather than, as might have been expected, against it. The general expectation of some kind of innovation in public affairs undoubtedly was present and contributed to the decision by so large a proportion of the electorate to 'try something new'. What is less clear is how far the change from 'old Labour' to 'New Labour' had an influence on the election. Lady Thatcher is reported to have remarked that 'they became electable through our beliefs'. This is a somewhat difficult sentence to understand, but it seems to say that the Labour Party achieved its electoral victory because it had embraced the policies of the Tory Party, particularly as conceived by the supposed author of this remark. Speculation about the extent to which the new direction of the Labour Party influenced the result must remain uncertain. The party, which had already tried to modernize itself during the preceding fifty years, nevertheless carried many of the barnacles of the old socialist tradition (British not Marxist).

Mr Blair did not quote St Francis on the steps of Number Ten when he took office. In a sense he had no need to stress the fact that his government was going to try to be the government for all the people. That seemed to be fairly generally accepted, something that is a relatively new phenomenon in British party politics.

PART TWO

Where We Are

Europe

I am departing at this stage from the strict pattern I have laid down and inserting a discussion on a subject that was of major importance in 'Where we were', continues to be so in 'Where we are' and will grow in its impact on all our affairs in the next two decades.

The problem of our relations with the rest of Europe deserves special treatment for a variety of reasons. In an earlier book to which I referred before, I characterized the European policy of successive British governments as one of the major errors responsible for a good deal of our lack of adequate economic performance. This went alongside, and was closely related to, the other great area of errors, namely that of exchange rate policy. It is, therefore, incumbent upon me to deal with this subject again to see how it is likely to be treated as a major policy ingredient by the new government.

The other reason is that it is a subject that will certainly be a fruitful source of debate between our country and other members of the European Union as well as of political controversy within our own country. It is almost certain to play an important part in the next election and in the subsequent policies of both parties. As far as the Liberal Democrats are concerned, I think they can for this purpose be left on one side, not because they are unimportant, but because their attitude is on the whole so plainly for full participation in European integration that we can confine our discussion to the other two political parties.

Although the new government in its electoral campaign, in its manifesto and in its early pronouncements has not taken an explicitly pro-European stand, it has certainly done its best to distance itself from the Euro-sceptic tendencies of its Conservative predecessors. It has also tried to subdue sceptical tendencies within its own party. Certainly in the broadest sense the Prime Minister and other major members of the government have consistently tried to identify themselves as 'good Europeans' without necessarily implying a favourable attitude to this or that major issue in European policy, with the exception – not surprisingly – of the Social Chapter. The Chancellor, although he too has been cautious, is thought to be even more pro-European than the Prime Minister. I think, however, that it would be wrong to draw a major distinction between them. The Foreign Secretary, while he was still in opposition, rightly or wrongly acquired the reputation of being something of a Euro-sceptic, though by no means an extreme one. Since becoming Foreign Secretary he also has characterized himself as a good European and has in fact made statements, including most recently about the possible reform of the European Parliament, that are designed to show him as being positive about European developments. Nevertheless, on some issues, notably the most urgent and central economic issue of all, the Single Currency and Economic and Monetary Union, he has been silent and is widely thought to be still somewhat sceptical.

The government is committed to take a decision on whether to join EMU after the next election and is also to have a referendum on the issue, when it will either recommend that Britain should join or not, as the case may be. Indeed, it is very likely that this will form a central issue in the election itself, particularly since the Conservative Party is at present committed not to join within this parliament or the next, in other words for nearly ten years.

In the meantime things have progressed. Eleven countries of the European Union have decided to go ahead with Economic and Monetary Union and to start by having a Single Currency on 1 January 1999. They have set up the European Central Bank and the System of European Central Banks around it, and the Central Bank is in fact already operating. It has its seat in Frankfurt, has appointed a President and an executive board and by all accounts the various questions of an operational character about its activities seem to be very much resolved or well on the way to resolution. Some specific issues concerning the relation of the members of the Single Currency and those outside – the UK, Denmark, Greece and Sweden – have apparently already been resolved or are still very actively being negotiated at present.

Most of the central banks of the member countries of the European Union, like the Federal Reserve in the United States, are now independent. That is to say they have independence of action in regard to monetary policy, which in most countries consists of the fixing of short-term interest rates. At the same time, in most countries, such as in our own, the Central Bank is supposed to be accountable for its actions. To whom it is accountable and in what manner this accountability is fulfilled, is not always the same, but practical means, such as reports to parliament or to parliamentary committees and appearance of the heads of the central banks before such committees, rather like that of the Chairman of the Federal Reserve Board before Congress, are common features.

The European Central Bank is also independent in the same way. Indeed, the independence of the European Central Bank has been strongly entrenched in the treaties that set it up as well as in the practical arrangements that have since been made. It is not very clear yet how the accountability of the European Central Bank will in fact be exercised, but ways and means of doing so in a practical manner can no doubt be found.

What is rather more difficult is a problem that has recently arisen and that is largely due to the change in the climate of economic thinking, which has taken place within the last year or two. Before then, the strong emphasis, both of governments and of central banks, was on the danger of inflation and the need to counter it. This meant an all-out effort to secure stability of prices and to practise fiscal rigour. That has recently changed. The Stability Pact under the Maastricht Treaty, which imposes a very strict fiscal regime on the members of the euro-zone, was another result of the fear of inflation that dominated economic thinking.

With the decline in economic growth the appearance of mass

unemployment – despite certain reductions here and there – now amounting to something like 16 million over the area of the European Union, has reawakened fears of deflation rather than inflation. I shall deal with this further in the sections concerned with monetary and fiscal policy. It is, however, of relevance here because it immediately raises certain questions about the relationship between the actions of the European Central Bank and the evident strong desire on the part of many members of the European Union to promote growth and employment. On a national level this has to be somehow or other sorted out between a Minister of Finance – in our case the Chancellor of the Exchequer – and the Governor of the Central Bank – or, in our case, the Monetary Policy Committee of the Central Bank – and is usually still characterized by strong emphasis on the independence of the bank and its role in preserving price stability. As far as the European Central Bank is concerned, no obvious mechanism exists. The euro-zone has eleven finance ministers, each still concerned with the finances of his own national territory. Now that the euro-zone has come into being and the Single Currency exists, the monetary policy of the euro-zone will inevitably be placed within the competence of the European Central Bank. However, any kind of co-ordinated or collective action or harmonization of action on the fiscal front has to be done by means of meetings of the eleven ministers of finance. In so far as those ministers may be, at least during the present period, primarily concerned with the promotion of growth and the reduction in unemployment, they have no ready means for co-ordinating anything they might wish to do with the monetary policy of the European Central Bank. This has given rise to considerable controversy already and to debate as to what to do about it. It is understood that a recent meeting of the eleven finance ministers was one in which they were unaccompanied, except by one silent note-taker each, and the meeting was therefore able to get down to much more intimate discussion of the problem in question. It is understood again that one or two of the members of that group have come away reasonably optimistic about reaching a collective view as to what is to be done if growth and employment are to be fostered. It remains to be seen how this problem will in fact be resolved in the months to come.

Select committees of the House of Commons and of the House of Lords have produced a large number of reports on various aspects of EMU, more particularly on the difficult question of whether Britain should join, and also what would be the relationship and the problems arising between the so-called 'ins' and the so-called 'outs', if we stayed out. Most recently the Select Committee of the House of Lords on European matters has also issued a report on the operation of the European Central Bank.

These economic and financial issues are undoubtedly the most immediate and will be the most pressing over the next couple of years as far as British policy is concerned. Of other matters, there are a number of important ones arising out of the Amsterdam intergovernmental conference and the agreements reached there. They concern to a large extent the structure of the European Union and the powers of its various constituent parts. Probably the most important and fundamental of these relates to the powers of the European Parliament. The controversy has turned primarily on whether the powers of the European Parliament are either excessive or adequately representative of the interests of all the members under the system of direct elections from individual special constituencies created for that purpose. There is a section of opinion in this country that is inclined to regard the European Parliament as an unnecessarily interfering body whose powers ought to be curbed. In fact, there is very little evidence that the powers of the European Parliament, either as they are drawn up in its constitution or as they have in fact been exercised since it came into existence, are such that they can effectively monitor the activities of the executive organs. Indeed, a good case can be made to show that it has had a relatively feeble influence in its relations with the 'executive' of the European Union, namely the European Commission, and with the representatives of the individual governments, as it is exercised in the Council of Ministers and in the occasional meetings at so-called summits.

This situation has recently shown signs of radical change as a result of the clash between the European Parliament and the Commission over cases of mismanagement and fraud that have come to light. Although the European Parliament did not press its case to the point of dismissing the whole Commission (the only sanction effectively open to it), nevertheless it has in the opinion of most observers emerged considerably strengthened. It may well be that this is the beginning of a major change in the balance of power between the different institutions of the European Union.

An interesting new suggestion as far as the European Parliament is concerned was made by the British Foreign Secretary in the summer of 1998, namely that the Parliament should be changed into a bicameral one with a second house, elected by the national parliaments of the member countries. It has been put forward – or at least it has been commented on in certain quarters – as essentially a proposal for curbing the powers of the directly elected European Parliament by bringing to bear upon it the additional deliberations and decisions of a body representative of national parliaments rather than a directly elected second chamber. This may be the intention. It has not been put in the forefront of the arguments in favour of this proposal by the British government itself, but it may well be so regarded by various people in the United Kingdom representative of different political opinions, and may indeed find some response in the views of public opinion generally in this country.

If this is really the intention, and if in practical working out it is going to be primarily oriented towards the purpose of putting a brake upon the directly elected European Parliament, it might well become the source of a good deal of controversy, not to say bickering, among the member countries. I myself believe that it is not only in itself a logical and interesting proposal, but that it may well turn out to have the opposite effect of what some at least of its protagonists might wish. In other words, it might produce a stronger European Union parliamentary ingredient than exists at the moment. The association of national legislators drawn from their own national parliaments with directly elected European Union parliamentarians, and obviously primarily concerned with European Union matters emerging either from the Council of Ministers, or more particularly from the Commission, could well create over time a much more closely knit, and therefore a much more effective, European Union governmental structure than exists now. It is certainly not a proposal that can be brushed aside, or that should be brushed aside.

The main trouble about it is that, emanating as it does from Britain, it is likely to create a suspicion that it is a diversionary tactic. Unfortunately in the past British proposals, or those supported by Britain, created that very suspicion – often justifiably. For example, under the previous administration, particularly under Mrs Thatcher, the great emphasis always put upon enlargement of the Community, at a time when strengthening existing ties and creating new ones, such as EMU, were very much to the fore in European Union discussions and debates, was considered a means of delaying and weakening the case for these closer ties. Enlargement and 'deepening', as it was called, were often regarded as alternatives, with Britain more on the side of enlargement precisely because it might at least delay deepening.

It would be very unfortunate if the proposal concerning the European Parliament, or any others that might emerge on the structural and constitutional front of the European Union, were to be regarded in the same light and either used, or at least suspected of being used, as means of enabling Britain to postpone a decision on what is more immediately on the agenda.

The case for Britain joining the Single Currency and the Economic and Monetary Union has been argued a great deal and need not be dealt with at great length. There are different levels of arguments both for and against. The most powerful argument against joining is not one that is easily analysed, because it rests essentially on emotions and a sort of residue of thinking not specifically related to the Single Currency but derived from broader considerations of national prestige, 'patriotism' and a general reluctance to change features of our society that have been

in existence for a very long time. These, as I say, are not suscep-
tible to specific rational arguments, but they are no less powerful
for that.

For example, one of the biggest problems that our government
would have to face were it to decide to go all out for joining
EMU is the opposition of very large sections of the media, not
only such tabloids as the *Sun*, but also two of our most established
'heavy' papers, *The Times* and the *Telegraph*. The arguments in
both these papers are that the suggestions for EMU participation
are not far removed from betrayal of British deep-seated national
institutions that should be preserved at all costs. Admittedly more
down-to-earth arguments are sometimes used, although not again
particularly argued. For example, the government has been
enjoined not to 'scrap the pound', which comes rather ironically
from a paper whose owner has shown more regard for the United
States dollar than for either the pound or his own original Austra-
lian currency. But leaving aside these arguments of emotion, there
are some sophisticated theories by some economists about what
constitutes an optimum currency area (significantly the leading
theorist of the optimum currency area is in favour of the euro) and
also about the relationship between political control of economic
arrangements and the technical features of those arrangements
themselves.

The argument is that British economic interests are very widespread, that they are in fact world-wide, and that our connections
either with the Commonwealth or with the newly emerging
markets of Eastern Europe, of Latin America or with the United
States are of such importance and magnitude that it would be
wrong to 'tie ourselves' to an exclusive currency club consisting
only of a dozen or so European members. This argument loses a
good deal of its strength when we look at the actual course of our
international trade and of our general economic and financial
relations world-wide. The members of the European Union now
form far the most important trading partners that we have. As
far as finance is concerned, of course there is absolutely no reason
why within the European Monetary Union, with the euro as the

common currency, we should not continue to exercise as much of our financial world-wide powers as we do now, or perhaps even more. Indeed, there is a good deal of indication already that the powers that we now have world-wide are being attacked by the euro and are in danger of eroding. This process is certain to increase as the powers of the institutions of the euro-zone, particularly the European Central Bank in Frankfurt, develop. There are already certain parts of our financial activities that are under considerable pressure from Frankfurt and Paris particularly, and to a much lesser degree from Amsterdam and Milan. While there is no reason to think that the City would not be able for some time to maintain its strong position even outside the EMU, the longer-term future is bound to be doubtful. The following factors operate in this respect: Frankfurt as the seat of the European Central Bank, monetary policy for the eleven members (plus any others that might eventually join the EMU) being determined at Frankfurt, exchange rate policy as an individual prerogative of each member country having disappeared and being merged in the exchange rate policy for the euro, and the capital market for the euro possibly developing more rapidly on the Continent than it has hitherto. It is highly probable that over a period of, say, five years there would be a migration of financial strength to the Continent. If the euro proves to be a reliable and strong currency with an exchange rate policy that should be relatively more easily handled vis-à-vis the dollar and with a possibility of actual agreements being reached with the monetary authorities of the United States (and Japan, if the yen becomes again a more important currency than it is at this moment), then sterling, which has long ago lost its pre-eminent position as a world trading currency to the US dollar, may find that the new Continental currency is a far stronger magnet both for capital formation and capital movements.

Certainly the possibility of the euro over time acquiring some of the advantages that the dollar has had in regard to the possibilities that its strength and its international position have opened up for the American balance of payments may well make us regret not sharing in that advantage by being part of the euro.

As far as the exchange rate policy is concerned, we have of course suffered a great deal already from having to handle this ourselves alone ever since we joined the European Exchange Rate Mechanism and then had to depart from it, not because it was in itself an unsuitable mechanism, as it is sometimes described, but because we had joined it at far too high an exchange rate. DM2.95 was certainly totally inappropriate at the time.

Of almost immediate concern, as far as Britain's entry into the Single Currency goes, is the effect it will have on the exchange rate. Our exchange rate policy – although policy is perhaps not quite the right word since it could be argued that the exchange rate has been determined indirectly as a consequence of monetary policy rather than as a direct objective of policy itself – has been widely criticized because it has kept the pound strong against our competitors. This has greatly damaged our export industries, has encouraged imports in competition with domestic production and has led to a general slow-down in manufacturing, and therefore in economic activity generally. The exchange rate has fluctuated since our departure from the Exchange Rate Mechanism, but it has generally been high, and there is no guarantee that it will not go even higher, as it has done on some occasions in the recent past.

Clearly belonging to a Single Currency, and thereby losing our own exchange rate policy, could be a way to divest ourselves of the consequences that either directly or indirectly flow from our monetary policy. Indeed, by joining the Single Currency we would not only cease to have an independent exchange rate, and therefore exchange rate policy, but we would also cease to have an independent monetary policy and be subject to the general monetary policy determined by the European Central Bank for the euro-zone as a whole. The consequences of such a change cannot be judged in the abstract. They would depend on how exactly the integration of our monetary and exchange rate policies into the policy for the euro-zone as a whole took place.

In this connection a certain amount of resistance to our joining the Single Currency has been derived from what I call the difficulties of convergence. Much has been made of the difference in our position in 'the economic cycle' as compared with that of our Continental partners. I think myself that this has been overdone. Indeed, the rediscovery recently of the economic cycle has itself to some extent been overdone. There are fluctuations; whether they are properly described as a cycle is by no means certain, nor is it quite clear whether it is necessary, or to what degree it is necessary, to have the same position in any system of fluctuation as that of our potential partners in the euro. If there are economic cycles, it is far from clear that ours, as compared with those of Germany, France, Belgium, Ireland etc., is significantly out of line. It is true that, leaving aside the broader question of the economic cycle, the actual level of our short-term interest rates and of our exchange rate is important. There is some difficulty with a short-term interest rate at our present level of $5\frac{1}{2}$ per cent and 3 per cent in the euro-zone to see how exactly this would be aligned. Some people fear that bringing our short-term interest rates into line, which membership of the euro-zone would involve, would be a very difficult matter, and if it were attempted over a short period could well regenerate inflationary pressures within the UK. This is a matter that is clearly much discussed in the inner circles of European central banks and treasuries and must be coming up for some definite policy decisions. It will require a certain amount of skilled management, which is the case for the whole range of banking policies and financial services generally in the whole euro-zone.

Relevant to this question is the broader question of what position the euro will occupy in the world currency arena. One can say that it will be the most important currency next to the dollar and possibly alongside the yen. The international status of the euro is a very interesting subject and it is as yet not quite certain how it will work out. It will clearly be dependent on how the world financial community, of which the financial services industries of the euro-zone themselves form a part, judges its economic, and more particularly its monetary, policy. In other words, it will depend on whether it considers the euro to be a strong, stable, reliable currency or not. In turn, the international status which the euro is able to build up for itself will have an influence on the range of options open to its own monetary authorities in regard to domestic monetary policy. This is clearly a reciprocal relationship of considerable intimacy.

A certain amount of discussion has already taken place as to whether the euro can achieve a position that would make it a potential alternative to the dollar, perhaps even a rival to the dollar, as an international trading currency and an international store of value. There is general agreement that the dollar's position as the premier trading and store-of-value currency in the world, which it acquired during and immediately after the First World War in replacement of the pound, has served the American economy very well indeed. Although not many people go as far as General de Gaulle – no economist he – who used to regard the American balance of payments as being a plaything for the American authorities precisely because of the international position of the dollar. He felt that the option of 'benign neglect', as it was called for a long period, was only open to the Americans because they were able to incur very substantial deficits internationally without suffering any immediate or even long-term domestic disadvantageous consequences from that situation. As a result of this line of argument the question is often asked whether the euro could also achieve a position of this kind, at least alongside the dollar, if not in replacement of it. There are a number of preconditions that have to be fulfilled if the euro is in fact to achieve that position. The political stability of the euro-zone is one. It may not be such as to be comparable to that of the United States, which is clearly without question politically stable whatever may happen in regard to the up and down of different political parties and movements within the country. Clearly the rather loosely-knit structure provided for the euro-zone by the institutions of the European Union, which extends beyond the immediate membership of the euro-zone, is hardly in the same class as a federal constitution and an established central government. Indeed, many of the existing members of the euro-zone, let alone those who stayed outside, notably the United Kingdom, have made the absence of such a political structure one of the preconditions for themselves if they were to contemplate joining a purely financial and economic arrangement, such as that of the Single Currency and EMU. Nevertheless, it is not excluded that, if the euro is a success within its own terms of reference, that may provide a sort of political cohesion strong enough to be perceived by the financial community as an adequate backing for the euro itself.

As regards the economic and financial status of the euro, there is no obvious reason why this should not be of a sufficiently high order to give the euro an important international role. After all, it brings together a number of currencies, notably the D-Mark, and to some degree the French franc, which are already playing a role, though a moderate one at this stage, as international currencies. It is sometimes thought that putting them altogether into the Single Currency pot would not necessarily produce a positive sum. What has so far been seen of the views of the leaders of the European Central Bank leads to the opposite conclusion.

In so far as the perception internationally of the 'solidity' of the euro is concerned, there is every indication that monetary policy is likely to be handled by the European Central Bank in a manner that will command confidence that they are maintaining a stable and strong currency. So to that extent the further requirement for international status will be met.

There is then the more difficult question as to what, apart from political stability and economic confidence, is necessary for a currency to become an international trading one and also an international store of value. History is not a complete guide to this. The origins of the international status of the pound, which lasted for so long, and then that of the dollar, which took over some eighty years or so ago, was undoubtedly to some extent, perhaps to a large extent, due to the high degree of capital formation in Britain in the first place, and later in the United

States, and the consequent substantial outflow of capital investment into other parts of the world in sterling and then in dollars. Whether the euro-zone will be capable of generating enough and also of exporting enough capital to have that additional support for its international status cannot as yet be clear. It is true that many of the constituent parts of the euro-zone are already fairly substantial exporters of capital, notably Germany, but also France, the Low Countries and Italy, and this would be very substantially enlarged if the United Kingdom were also to join, plus of course Sweden and Denmark. Greece would hardly count in this particular context. Even on the basis of eleven members, the potential for capital formation and capital export is substantial; an enlargement of the euro-zone, in the first instance to those existing members of the Union who are not yet members, particularly the United Kingdom, would make a substantial difference.

Taking it all in all, there is considerable potential here for the euro's future as an international currency. It is significant that already in the first few months of its existence more than half of the international bond issues launched were denominated in euros. It is sometimes suspected that the overt or more frequently hidden scepticism in the United States, not to say antagonism towards the European Single Currency, is in part due to a fear of substantial competition in regard to the international status between the euro and the dollar. The supremacy of the dollar, as I have said, has undoubtedly already made many policy problems for the United States easier than they would otherwise have been.

Of course the case for British entry after all is said and done remains a debatable one, although it is significant that a large part of the City and of big industry is greatly in favour of our joining, while the political parties remain divided. As far as the Conservatives are concerned, there are those, led again by Mrs Thatcher, who would wish to extend the ban on joining beyond even the two parliaments that the Conservative leader has stipulated and make it a permanent ban – whatever permanence may mean in matters of this kind.

I close this particular discussion on a positive note. I am myself convinced that it would be right for us to join as soon as the political circumstances permit, which could be very much influenced by the determination of the government itself. I also think that this would be very much to our advantage and that it would enable us to play a leading part within the European Union much greater than the role that is open to us so long as we stay out of the Single Currency and EMU.

Moreover, it is not easy to see in what directions the European Union as such could develop and achieve a much more substantial status in world affairs without the creation of Economic and Monetary Union. It certainly has not covered itself with glory in the few attempts it has made to act as an entity in international conflicts such as in Yugoslavia, or in regard to major international difficulties such as the Middle East situation or Iraq. Whether one wishes these feeble attempts to be greatly strengthened and enlarged is obviously a matter of debate, but certainly if those who are against our joining EMU and making EMU a very important part, perhaps the most important part, of the European Union's *raison d'être* in the world, are looking for anything else that would take its place, it is very difficult to see what that might be. Enlargement to include other countries not at present in the European Union would be a desirable step and would certainly strengthen the Union, but again primarily in regard to economic matters, which are indeed the ones that attract the potential new members in Central and Eastern Europe more than anything else.

On that account also there is everything to be said for the United Kingdom being right in the heart of what must be the most important single development of the European Union, namely that in the currency and economic fields.

Britain's entry into the Single Currency and into EMU, say, within the next two years or so, would bring to a happy end the unfortunate chapter that, starting at least at the end of the War, if not before, has consistently, in my opinion, weakened, if not bedevilled, British policy, economic and otherwise.

As far as attitude to Europe is concerned, it will be interesting to see how the two major political parties line up for the next election in defining their positions. I have already said much about Labour, and although it is not possible yet to be certain about the eventual stance of the party in regard to Europe, the chances are that it will be broadly in favour and may in fact go so far as to recommend, perhaps even during the election, but certainly in the subsequent referendum, that Britain should join the common currency and EMU.

The Tories as of now would of course oppose that, and if they follow the injunctions of Lady Thatcher, they will even make their stance more rigid and definitely hostile to any further European monetary integration. It may well be that this will turn out to be the only major policy issue on which the Tories will have a distinct attitude and programme. It is very difficult to see that they can make much of the relatively less high-tensioned differences that divide them from Labour on a number of practical issues, such as taxation or even welfare. In fact, if the Euro-antagonists (which is what the Euro-sceptics have now turned out to be) have their way, it may well be that the anti-European attitude of the Conservative Party will have a strong tinge of a more general xenophobic character than is now the case. What that will do as far as its impact on the electorate is concerned is hard to say, but it is difficult to believe that the broad British public will take kindly to a xenophobic programme unless of course the general economic situation, and with it social and political attitudes, have become considerably more acerbic than they are today.

The alternative that might attract the Tory programme-makers is a strong leaning towards the United States, in other words almost amounting to embracing the option, which has lately been propagated by one media tycoon of Canadian origin, of 'choosing America' rather than Europe. This, in the opinion of many people, and certainly of this author, is totally illusory even if it were desirable. It is very difficult to see that Britain joining NAFTA, which is a North American-Mexican free trade area arrangement, would be particularly acceptable to the United States except on terms that would turn Britain quite openly and definitively into an economic satellite. The political implications of this, quite apart from the economic ones, could be very substantial and it is not clear that the British electorate would readily take to such a position. Even in the heyday of our alliance just after the War, when Britain and the United States were the major Western nuclear powers – as at the moment they still are – the taunt that Britain was in danger of becoming, as it were, an American aircraft carrier was enough to turn many people into sceptics. The friendship, attraction and attachment to the United States in our country is great, and rightly so, but there is an enormous step both in terms of wishes and in terms of practicability between that and actually lining up with the United States economically, beginning with trade and currency and going on to broader matters. Quite apart from that, the existing links within the European Union, even without the additional link of the Single Currency, have become so strong that it is almost inconceivable that they could be easily unravelled and replaced by some kind of jointure with the States of the American Union of which Britain would then become virtually the fifty-first.

The proposal to join NAFTA or in some other way 'choosing' attachment to the United States instead of further development of the European Union is at the moment confined to relatively few people in this country. It is the hobby of a powerful media magnate, and this power obviously should not be underestimated. On the other hand, I am old enough, and possibly some of my readers are old enough, to remember the little man dressed in knight's armour and appearing in red on the masthead of a popular paper – at that time a broadsheet – some sixty years ago or more. It symbolized the 'Empire Crusade', of which a powerful media magnate at that time – oddly enough also originating from Canada – was the author. I do not think the Empire Crusade, which at that time had far stronger ideological and emotional roots within this country than attachment to the United States would have now, got very far. Indeed, developments in Europe, the rise of the dictators, the outbreak of war and other developments subsequently completely changed the picture. Despite the strong

35

signals that our present Prime Minister has sent across the Atlantic, both towards the United States generally and more particularly towards its present President, I doubt very much whether the government itself would easily be won over to a so-to-speak pro-American, anti-European stance.

An Overview

Before I look at the problems facing the new government, some preliminary remarks on the broader constraints on government – any government – policy are necessary.

Throughout this century, the weight of influences outside our own shores upon our fortunes has been growing steadily. Today, and looking ahead to the next twenty years, the list is longer than ever and its weight formidable. To look first at the strongest economy of all, that of the United States, we see developments the precise outcome of which is not as yet easily assessed. The United States has succeeded in the last decade or so in subduing inflation despite continued growth, and overcoming a fairly long period of unemployment through the creation of new jobs. At the same time and in spite of certain fears that are currently being raised, the danger of deflation is still not very obvious, so that the balancing act of monetary stability with continued growth is still one of the more favourable developments on the world economic scene. However, even here there are signs that a price has had to be paid for this relatively fortunate state of affairs. The disparity between the rich and the poor has grown greatly. It is in some estimates stated that there are hundreds of thousands of millionaires in the United States and something like 150 billionaires. This, even with the successful and continuing growing propensity towards philanthropy through the creation of foundations of all kinds – some for somewhat dubious purposes – is nevertheless a potentially destabilizing factor in the economy. This is particularly so since, though poverty on a very large and wide scale has been somewhat diminished, there are still many very poor urban areas and particularly pockets of gross poverty among the black communities in urban areas. It is true that the United States has managed in part to reconstruct and reform its welfare system, for example in New York City, to provide alternatives that this country will be looking at, so as to create work opportunities and alternatives to the passive receipt of social benefit payments. Still, the balance of the economy can never be absolutely assured and falling back into inflation or falling forward into deflation are both possible. This is strengthened by the accumulation of private wealth, which produces not only social but also economic and financial problems of its own.

In Europe, the economic strength of the individual countries that make up the European Union, even those that have been most successful in the past such as Germany, that of those in Central Europe that are on the threshold of joining it and, to some extent, that of the northern countries too, is by no means completely assured. Certainly, as for the individual economies, none of them plays a decisive or even a very significant part in fashioning the course of the world economy. Russia, a large and potentially very substantial economy, is still labouring under many difficulties. These stem from the consequences of a less orderly administrative apparatus than under the previous system, yet at the same time combined with the appearance of economic liberalism. This has produced crime and corruption, which no doubt our own economies experienced when they were emerging into modern capitalism.

On the other side of the world, in the Pacific area, the second strongest economy in the world, Japan, has suffered very substantial problems in recent years. They are most marked in the financial system, where they have already led to important bankruptcies in banking and in the brokerage houses, and where the tale is by no means at an end. The industrial economy has shown greater resilience, though here too the consequences of the heavy burden of unproductive loans by the financial system, the volatility of share prices and in recent times their substantial decline, have meant extremely difficult problems also for the large industrial and trading corporations. Furthermore the whole macro-economic environment, particularly as it affects exchange rates, the competitiveness of the Japanese economy and the balance between foreign trade and domestic demand, is certainly giving rise to considerable uncertainties.

In the rest of the Asian and Pacific area, recent turmoil has demonstrated the precarious nature of the great advances that seem to have been achieved in countries such as Indonesia, Malaysia and Thailand, to some extent even in Taiwan. So far, China, by far the largest country in the world with a $1\frac{1}{4}$ billion population, enormous natural resources and a record in the last fifteen years of very substantial economic growth, has managed to escape the worst of the financial, trading and industrial turbulence of the rest of South-East Asia. But here too there are some considerable uncertainties about the future. The incorporation of Hong Kong, which was at last achieved in 1997, has undoubtedly added important assets to the Chinese economic apparatus in the international field, but with it also greater exposure to the kind of financial upheaval that the rest of South-East Asia has already suffered. So far at any rate the determination of the Chinese authorities to reduce excessive economic growth (the present target being somewhere between 7 and 8 per cent, compared with 12 and more in the most recent past), and to maintain the exchange value of the Chinese currency as well as the peg of the Hong Kong dollar to the American dollar, has been well managed. One cannot be certain that this determination alone will continue to be effective. The pressures are undoubtedly very considerable and the excessive economic growth in the most recent past has left much of the industrial apparatus, including particularly the three hundred thousand or so state enterprises, in an extremely exposed position. The banking system too, which has largely financed the growth of these enterprises, may suffer from much the same difficulties that for example the Japanese financial system has suffered, but these of course are not as visible, given the kind of political and administrative apparatus that envelops it in China.

A recital – by no means complete – of some of these factors of the external environment that will be continuing to operate from time to time in a largely unforeseeable manner during the next twenty years shows how very little influence we – and indeed most of the individual European countries by themselves – can have on much that will influence their own development. Against this background and looking at the world situation, it is quite clear that this country is now a relatively modest player on the world scene with little, if any, influence on much of the broad development that I have described.

In one field, financial services of all kinds – insurance and so on, but also particularly in the banking and capital markets, investment and fund management – Britain is sometimes a leading player, often the premier one in the world, and to that extent has an influence beyond much of its other economic assets. Therefore it could be said that so far as financial developments will mark the surrounding economic and political environment in which our country operates, Britain may play, for some time at least, an active and occasionally a decisive part.

Even in this connection, however, it should be noted that this asset may not always be of the strength that it has been for nearly two centuries. The coming of the Single Currency as the start of the Economic and Monetary Union, from which Britain on present form will remain excluded for at least four years, will undoubtedly change the power relationships even in regard to finance between different countries. It may well be that while London continues to preserve its strength for some years, by the time we are ready to enter the Economic and Monetary Union (if we do!), the then existing Union, including the euro as its currency, will have progressed considerably and it will be very difficult indeed for us at that stage to be able to exercise a major influence on the subsequent course of events.

However, even when our relative strength for some time in the future is taken into account, it is clear that much of the best that our government will be able to do over the next twenty years will largely be to react in the most appropriate manner possible to influences coming from the outside. From a positive, or what is nowadays called a proactive, point of view our fortunes will be largely determined by what we do for ourselves within our own economy. It is perhaps an ironic fact that the external influences that are closest to our own, namely those of Europe, are precisely the ones that through the misjudgements of past governments have been neglected, and have been allowed to develop in a way on which we ourselves have little influence. One of the points that I shall be discussing later will be precisely how far the new government, both by what it has already demonstrated and by what it is likely to be compelled to do in regard to Europe, can remedy that situation and how far Europe on a more united basis can intervene more effectively in world events that are so important to its own fortunes.

A New Broom

The government elected on 1 May 1997 with an enormous majority, unprecedented certainly this century, has been in office at the time I write this for eighteen months. No definite judgement can yet be made of its performance to date, let alone of its future, even though it has itself issued a report (one of its proud innovations) on its initial stewardship. It came into power with a fanfare of trumpets, as was not surprising after eighteen years in the wilderness, and with a claim to be different from the Labour Party as it was known until only two decades earlier. Its first 100 days were much celebrated by the party faithful. There is a natural temptation to compare it with the 100 days of Harold Wilson's administration, also a Labour government that had come into office after a long period, that time only twelve years, of Tory rule.

The Wilsonian Labour Party was still very much the old one. There were members in the government who were ready to strike out anew. George Brown, despite a certain wayward temperament in many respects, was also, perhaps for that very reason, less ready to follow old doctrines. For example, in regard to nationalization of industries he displayed a fresh mind and fresh ideas. Jim Callaghan had been preparing himself for the office of Chancellor by imbibing substantial doses of modern economics and Keynesian ideas (which, as anybody who has really studied them knows, were far from being 'anti-capitalist'). Still, the general character of the party and the government was unmistakably the old one. There was perhaps not so much a real, but still a very much perceived, hostility to 'business'. Certainly some of the advisers who, as a result of the 1964 election victory, became attached to government, were not only suspicious of business but often antagonistic to it. This was part of a sort of general tradition of hostility to the 'establishment' that had grown up in the latter years of Labour's period in the wilderness. Establishment was an ill-defined term and used freely to attack whatever happened to be at the moment prominently within the sights of that particular segment of the Labour Party and the Labour leadership.

Some further comparison of the New Labour government with that of Harold Wilson is interesting: it shows some similarities but also considerable differences. The main similarities are that each came into office after a very prolonged period of Conservative government; in both cases there was a spirit of innovation and renewal in the air; each was heralded by great expectations, both from itself and from its followers, but also to a considerable extent from the country at large. The main difference, as I have already pointed out, was in the size of the majority, exiguous in Harold Wilson's case and enormous in that of Tony Blair. Furthermore, whereas Harold Wilson came into office as leader of the Labour Party after a prolonged and fairly bitter battle for the leadership and for the succession to Hugh Gaitskell, who never got to the top, in the present case the succession of Tony Blair to the prematurely departed John Smith appears to have been without significant difference. The likely candidature of Gordon Brown was quickly abandoned by himself, though subsequent rumours suggest some remaining discontent at the top. Now, eighteen months after the election, these rumours imply that the resolution of the leadership question was not as smooth as it seemed. The rumours have resurfaced more strongly after the first Cabinet reshuffle. However, even if the rumours carry some truth, there can be no comparison with the 1963/64 situation. Tony Blair came into office without any major open rivalries still surrounding him at the very top of the Cabinet. This was certainly not the case in Harold Wilson's time, when both Callaghan and Brown had been very close contenders; and to some extent the disappointment it created for the two of them and the differences between them remained operative even after the party came into power. It had some influence on changes in the machinery of governments, which I deal with in a more general way later.

Another point worth mentioning is that whereas the Wilson administration contained a number of members who had already had governmental experience (though some years back) as well as Civil Service experience during and after the war (with at least the advantage of knowledge of the 'machine'), the Blair government is practically devoid of this. Its experience is virtually confined to opposition politics in parliament and the country. Then again the basic outlook and programme, both longer term and for the immediate future of the party, were very different. Harold Wilson carried still a very large ballast of old socialist policy, including Clause 4, and with it also considerable difficulties in regard to defence and foreign policy, which it took him some time to overcome. In this respect, and also in regard to the respective roles of the State and of private enterprise, there were – apparently at least – no very acute issues for Tony Blair when he came into office. Thus it can be said that his insistence on New Labour and the new outlook and programme of the party were in line with much of the thinking in the country, although no real definition of 'New' Labour has been forthcoming.

One other very important difference was that Harold Wilson's room for manoeuvre was greatly constrained not only by the size of his majority but also by the very critical state in which the final stages of Tory government had left the economy, particularly as far as the balance of payments was concerned. He was faced with a raging balance of payments crisis and continued attacks on sterling, creating the need to be constantly mindful of the attitudes, opinions and powers of world financial markets as well as of the international financial institutions, particularly the International Monetary Fund, to which the country was very likely to have recourse during the critical period ahead. None of these situations threatened the Blair administration. Whatever may be the weaknesses of the economy, and whatever may be the difficulties of the external situation, particularly in regard to the consequences of the high exchange value of the pound both for monetary policy domestically and for our international trade position, there certainly was no immediate critical situation facing the monetary authorities, though on economic policy as a whole some troublesome hints of an impending recession are disturbing. In short, therefore, to a very large extent the room for manoeuvre of the Blair administration is great and practically unprecedented since the end of the Second World War. The main constraint comes, oddly it may seem, primarily from the government and the party itself and – in a much more distant sense – in the effect it has on public opinion and its possible influence when the time for the next election comes round, say in 2002.

I have referred to the speculation concerning the factors that went to make up the unexpected and, in its size, extraordinary victory; but in fact this speculation is of very little consequence except for historians and specialists in psephology. What is far more important is what is now going to be the use to which this majority is going to be put. This book is concerned with where this country ought to be going in the next two decades in the light of the present situation and the problems of the recent past, and also where this country is likely to be going given the kind of government it is going to have in all probability for at least half that period.

In looking ahead, I will leave out very large and important areas of public policy that would require far more extensive treatment than I can give them here. I will concentrate very much on economico-political affairs, particularly in so far as they can be determined or at least significantly affected by the actions of government, and only incidentally refer to other factors, such as scientific and technological development that will affect the economy. I will leave out the following without in any way suggesting that they are not only highly important in themselves, or that they will not have an influence on matters with which I am going to deal in the following pages. The fabric – social, political and cultural – of a complex modern society like ours is a seamless web and anything of any importance that affects any one part of it is bound to affect the whole; but in the end an analytical enquiry

45

has to proceed by selection and abstraction and hence the choice that I am making here.

Of the topics which I am not dealing with at all I would mention first of all the cultural factors, as these are more distantly related to economic and economico–political developments. They are certainly not unimportant and by no means entirely irrelevant to the economy. Changes may well take place in the organization of the arts, both creative and expository: the future of our museums, the financing of the arts from public funds or quasi-public funds or national lotteries and so on, or the future of the Arts Council. All these matters are still very much under debate at the moment. I will not say that they are without significance for the economy or our political life, but they are much less directly related.

In the legal field, the most closely related is the possible revision of company law and all that is connected with the organization and functioning of corporations. Company law has undergone a number of changes in recent decades, but basically it is still as it emerged after the War in the Companies Act of 1948. Recent developments and reports on what is now fashionably called 'corporate governance' by the Cadbury Committee, the Greenbury report and the reports of the Hampel Committee, will all influence thinking in this regard. The experiences with certain cases of malpractice, fraudulent behaviour and the attempt to stamp out insider dealing by the existing criminal law changes in that regard, have all shown the need for a more comprehensive review of the system. Obviously this will have quite an important influence on the conduct of economic life, but again it is of a highly specialized character and not suitable to be dealt with inside the framework that I have described.

Further afield still are the changes in the criminal law and in the structure, administration and practice of the judiciary, where there have been a number of highly controversial attempts by the last government, not all of which have been found in the end acceptable by parliament. These go very deeply into the social structure and conditions of the State, but again they are of too highly specialized a character to be dealt with here.

Other matters that cannot be dealt with in detail, but which I shall be touching upon, relate to constitutional matters. The government has instituted a review of the electoral system, which may in the end produce something very different from what has been in operation for so long, namely the 'first past the post system'. If some kind of proportional representation system is adopted, it will undoubtedly in the longer term change the political map of the country; but this again is very uncertain. More immediately relevant is the reform of parliament through changes in the House of Lords. The government is committed to do something here, but it is by no means clear yet what exactly this will be. The disappearance of the hereditary principle to all intents and purposes is almost certain to take place. Whether larger reform will be accomplished before the next parliament, or will take longer, remains to be seen. There may well be transitional periods. My own guess would be that a mixture between life peers and some beginnings of an elected element may be adopted, though any elected element will raise the question of the powers of the new House.

Other developments of a more general character, which will certainly be taking place within the next twenty years, are changes in the educational system, in regard both to structure, funding and curricula. The present situation is by all accounts unsatisfactory and it is not clear whether the government has yet made up its mind in which directions remedies are to be sought. Leaving aside the more complex and technical elements of the curriculum, the relationship between primary, secondary and higher education and the relation of all this to research, there is the more pervasive problem of the sheer penury of teachers, both in numbers and perhaps even, in some stages, in quality. It is very difficult to see how this can be remedied simply by administrative reform and without a very substantial change in funding, which almost inevitably must result in the total expenditure on education being increased, even though some realignment of funds between different stages and administration could provide relief. These matters I can only touch upon very briefly.

Similarly the changes in the National Health Service, which have already begun with the virtual abolition of the misguided reforms of the last governments in regard to trusts, internal budgets, competition and all the rest of it, are by no means clear yet. One of the enormous difficulties in this area is that both the demand for health services and care and the supply – that is to say the possibilities now available – have increased greatly. The ageing of the population and the change in its structure, as well as the self-propelling factors of higher education and greater requirements in regard to standards of living, have produced a considerable increase in the demand for both medical and surgical services.

On the supply side the progress in the production of drugs of all kinds and in surgical procedures has again enlarged the possibilities for taking care of disease and both curing or ameliorating diseases and prolonging life. This of course cannot be achieved in practice without greater expenditure of funds. For drugs alone, it was estimated not long ago, it takes about twelve years from original research to the actual marketing of a new compound; and that means of course the use of a very substantial machine of research, basic and clinical, and trials of all kinds, all of which require a great deal of expenditure. The relationship between the great pharmaceutical companies of the world – one of the industries that has undergone substantial changes, and there is no doubt that these will continue on a massive scale – has shown that there is a big problem here in deciding to what extent the costs of bringing new compounds to the market justify the high profits of the big pharmaceutical companies and what savings could be made here without endangering the further progress of research, since in all countries there is some degree, sometimes a very substantial degree, of public provision of medicaments. This of course immediately raises the very difficult problem in regard to public expenditure and the extent to which health should be provided for in national budgets.

48

In regard to all these matters, in preparation for the election, during the election campaign and in its first weeks of office, the new government showed itself – and this was to all appearances deliberate – quite different in attitude from the old Labour Party. Indeed this went so far that many left-wing elements of the party felt not only that old principles and beliefs were endangered – had even been betrayed – but that the party as it presented itself to the electorate had moved so close to the ideas of its opponents that it would be difficult to distinguish between the two.

Whatever explanations may evolve about reasons for the outcome of the 1997 election, it certainly did not in any way reflect the fears that had been held in sections of the Labour Party. The apparent closeness in ideas, particularly economic ideas, to those of their predecessors did not stand in the way of their gaining a huge vote from the electorate. The causal relationship between the two, however, is by no means clear, although, as I have mentioned, Margaret Thatcher thought they were related.

Much of the pre-election propaganda, and particularly the campaign oratory, put the emphasis on the novelty of the party compared with its forefathers, but this was not defined in precise terms. No doubt this was inevitable because it is an old prescription in political debate, particularly for a party that has been out of power for a long time, not to be too precise in its programme and pledges until it has in fact been elected, taken office and, as the saying goes, had a chance 'to look at the books'. However, in some respects the commitments during the election campaign in particular were quite precise. Oddly enough these were largely in the field of economic policy, and particularly in fiscal and monetary policy. In the former, the party leadership committed itself to maintaining the total spending programme roughly speaking as it had been established by their predecessors and also undertook not to raise the rates of personal taxation. There were no pledges in regard to indirect taxation, particularly VAT, and it was widely thought that the party would not be able to avoid making some changes, particularly in such areas as taxation of fuel, which would hit the poorer sections of the population very hard.

In regard to the welfare provision, social services generally and benefits of all kinds, the general impression conveyed during the election was that the party was pledged, broadly speaking, to maintaining 'the welfare state' and to being generally more benevolent towards the maintenance of benefits for the underprivileged, but without any very specific commitments. Similarly, in regard to the great expenditure items, education and the National Health Service, there were no precise commitments at that stage.

The commitment to keep – at least for some time – within the Tory government's spending limits was, not surprisingly, much criticized by the more old-fashioned (or more left-wing) elements in the party. It was said to be both unnecessary and contrary to tradition. On the other hand, it could be, and has been, argued that having been out of power for so long and having attacked a good deal of the policy in regard to expenditure and taxation of its predecessors, the government could be faced immediately on coming into power with an enormous list of very substantial demands for improvements here and there. This inevitably could not be fulfilled without very radical realignment of taxation and of spending in other respects.

Accordingly many felt, as I did, that the government was wise to secure for itself a substantial breathing space before opening the door to claims for specific improvements or for radical alterations in spending, which might also carry with them changes in taxation. In the Queen's Speech the government did commit itself to a review of these matters and in fact has since embarked on a series of reviews of both great length and depth in all sorts of subjects ranging from criminal justice to social benefits.

After eighteen months it is difficult to weigh up these various statements and tendencies against each other and seek to arrive at some kind of a balanced view of where the new government is likely to go. This is partly so since the government has a very large majority at its disposal and this, as experience has shown, is not only a solid foundation for legislation and action of all kinds, but also contains quite substantial dangers of gradually developing centrifugal tendencies. The government also has a substantial period in office ahead of it. It certainly has one whole parliament and need not bother about an election until 2002. Given the size of its majority, it is not an unreasonable assumption that unless there is some catastrophic outside development in world affairs or an exceptionally grievous error by the government, the danger lies in internal dissension rather than in a disappearance of the majority over its opponents within five years. So taking it all in all one could assume that New Labour is now in power for ten years. Hazardous though such an assumption is, it does mean that in the evolution and execution of its programme, the government can take a certain amount of time for considering and deciding on long-term action and long-term reform as indeed, judging by the list of the 'reviews' that have been instituted, it intends to do.

However, the internal doubts leading to possible dissension have not disappeared. Already the Chancellor in particular, given that he was the main proponent of the spending and taxation commitments during the election, has been involved in a certain amount of controversy with outside opinion as well as with older party members, including former ministers.

Much of the criticism of his immediate action, and even more so of his statements of policy, have been inspired by very long-standing, indeed ancient, 'socialist' principles and ideas, particularly egalitarianism. The Chancellor has defended his position by arguing that the essential objective of the government was to create equality of opportunity and not to be concerned about equality of 'outcome'. Leaving aside the rather curious new term – which is clearly designed to avoid getting into an argument about 'income' and what 'merits' this or that income is based on – the position is in itself not unreasonable, and the objective of equality of opportunity is such that it has even been accepted by the opposing party as a worthy characteristic of a decent society.

However, against this argument has been put the problem of immediate concern, namely the continued existence of poverty, and indeed in some respects its aggravation in recent years, together with the very great disparities of income and wealth, which have also grown and which cannot always be justified on grounds of merit or by special contributions to the common weal for those who have been fortunate enough to be at the top end.

It is unlikely that this argument will disappear from the political agenda. The doubts concerning the current direction are not confined to the extreme left-wing elements of the Labour Party or the unreconstructed 'old' Labour supporters. The argument for relying primarily on equality of opportunity requires substantial reforms and improvements in the education system, recruitment and training, together with the measures designed to make a genuine and lasting dent in unemployment. The trouble is that the reforms take time and the impatience of those who have been criticizing the government is no doubt due to the fact that many of the current flaws and blemishes of our society are very obvious and very repugnant. Much patience would be required, and the critics might say with Andrew Marvell, 'Had we but world enough and time . . .' Moreover, in the face of these inequalities, it is not easy to argue effectively for 'wage restraint', one of the factors thought essential in the continued fight to contain inflation.

The other factor is that we do not start with a clean sheet in creating a situation that would, through increased equality of opportunity, justify differences in what Gordon Brown has now called 'outcome'. The existing inequalities are far from being always justifiable and if the reforms that would eventually create a more acceptable society take too long, the short-term flaws would continue, could worsen and might become irrevocable and intolerable.

Before proceeding to consider the actual policies of the government and their consequences, including the macro–economic ones, it is necessary to look at the political philosophy of the government in more detail.

I begin by looking at it in the most abstract sense without specific regard either to what the party appears to have stood for during the campaign that brought it to victory or to what it has done since either in pronouncements of intentions or in actual action and achievement, legislative and otherwise. I want rather to look at what in the abstract might be achieved or, at least, expected.

The first thing to notice is that in terms of personnel it is considerably different from what has gone before. First of all, the average age of the leading figures is lower. The leader himself, the present Prime Minister, is younger than most of his predecessors of either party; although Harold Wilson was not very different in age, he had longer to prepare for office and actually to be in office. He also had wartime experience in the Civil Service, which he shared with many others of his colleagues. But more generally, Blair is a different type from the leaders of the last sixty years or so. The great figures of the Labour movement and of Labour governments before, during and immediately after the War, include Ernie Bevin, very much the old type of trade union leader – the 'dockers' KC' as he was known in earlier days – who brought to high office, particularly as Minister of Labour during the War, experience and skill in implementing the necessary mobilization of labour. As Foreign Secretary after the war he was imbued with a simple spirit of fairness and patriotism, which at the same time did not ignore the realities of other countries' interests.

Herbert Morrison had a great deal of governmental experience, but was also schooled in London municipal politics, which made him in the eyes of some people a magnificent 'fixer', but in the eyes of others an extremely realistic and accomplished political operator. Stafford Cripps was quite different from the others: an intellectual, a distinguished lawyer, son of a large upper-middle-class family that had experience in many aspects of public life, and a man of strong socialist convictions. Attlee, somewhat similar in social origins to Cripps, had a good deal of experience in local politics and local government, but also in voluntary organizations in the whole of the Toynbee Hall tradition of doing good. He had considerable management ability and ruled his cabinet by all accounts with skill, but also with great authority and little tolerance for extravaganzas.

The personalities that began to come to the fore in the first post-war Labour government, and even more so thereafter, although they still shared very much the intellectual origins of their predecessors, were a distinctly different breed in many ways. They were younger; they had been schooled in both the administrative and the economico-theoretical principles of the war-time Labour experience; they had come under the influence of Keynes and, as it must be remembered all the time, were already determined to move away from the war-time type of command economy into rather freer, but still regulated, areas. It must also be remembered that it was the younger members, Harold Wilson himself in the lead, who made a 'bonfire of controls' during the first experience of Labour governments from 1945 to 1951. Some displayed even more innovative spirits. Hugh Gaitskell, and his friend and companion Evan Durbin, who died tragically too young to occupy an important post, were outstanding in this area. They shared 'socialist convictions' with which they had grown up, but it must be remembered, for example, that Hugh Gaitskell was very much a modern trained economist, fully schooled in the theories of capital and interest of Böhm-Bawerk and the Vienna School, with full knowledge of Keynesian economics, although by no means exclusively devoted to them. He had great experience and a considerable respect for the achievements of Continental social democracy, especially in the housing policies of the pre-war Vienna Social Democrats.

The untimely death of Hugh Gaitskell had two unfortunate consequences. It deprived the party of a leader who was perhaps particularly suitable to lead the transition to what might have emerged with much similarity to today's New Labour.

The second consequence was that, as I have already said, it led to a quite acute struggle for the leadership, which finally went to Harold Wilson, who then led the party to victory in the election. The struggle left serious marks of contention and disagreement within the government. The three contenders – Harold Wilson,

Jim Callaghan and George Brown – managed to establish a certain equilibrium in running the government despite its minuscule majority after the 1964 election. However, disagreements remained and contributed to the confusion of policy. George Brown, who had had governmental experience as a junior minister in the Ministry of Agriculture, was a man of exceptional intelligence, but of a very uncertain temperament, given to occasional turbulent manifestations. He was remarkably free from ideology despite his deep roots in the Labour movement and substantial contacts in the trade unions. He was open-minded in regard to nationalization and other firmly established dogmas of the party and indeed would have led a 'business-friendly' policy at the time.

Jim Callaghan had a much more equable temperament and clearer conduct towards colleagues, opponents and the general public, and as he showed subsequently when he became leader and Prime Minister, was able to command a considerable degree of consensus.

Harold Wilson, a man of great talent, considerable experience in academic life, in the war-time Civil Service and then in politics, suffered unfortunately from something which is often present in members of the Left, particularly those who come from an intellectual background into practical politics, namely a belief that successful politics requires a great deal of manoeuvring and 'fixing'. He also suffered from that occupational disease, a tremendous regard for the PR aspects of leadership. This showed itself for example in that he was never really without his PR man, Joe Haines, at his elbow. Almost immediately after any decision or meeting or anything of that kind, the first question was: 'How do you present this to the public?' No doubt a good deal of this is inevitable, but an excess of it can be very debilitating in the longer run, as indeed Harold Wilson himself discovered.

This little disquisition on the leaders of the Labour government of the sixties and seventies is of some use, I think, to provide a comparison with the present leadership of New Labour and the government that we have today. The first thing that is clear is that in so far as 'New' Labour represents some breach with the past, it is not entirely new. The group of politicians who came to the fore in the sixties and seventies, admittedly after a little interval of Michael Foot, were very different in general formation, in their basic policy doctrines and also in their responses to the changing needs of the British economy and of the world situation. To that extent they can be regarded as at least the forerunners, if not themselves members, of a kind of new Labour Party.

The second thing about the Labour government as we have it today is that the content of 'New' has not to this day been adequately defined. This is perhaps not surprising and one might even say it is natural. It is never absolutely wise and can often be extremely hazardous for a party, particularly when it has been out of power for a long time, to define too precisely what it stands for, to clothe itself in carefully tailored ideological garments and to define precisely what its programme and objectives will be. To ask for that would be to ask for something that is possibly desirable, but successful only at certain times in the history of our political system. It certainly would not have been particularly helpful to the Labour Party in gaining an electoral victory in 1997 had it done so. However, the fact remains that the absence of a clear definition of 'new' is somewhat frustrating. This is not sufficiently counterbalanced by pointing to specific things ranging from the reform of the criminal justice system to the new status of the Bank of England or to the new techniques of determining the government's taxing and spending programmes. There are some sources here and there that enable one to construct a rather fragmentary picture of the broader doctrinal, not to say ideological, character of the present Labour Party as seen by its leaders. There is, for example, a book written before the election by one of the members of the Cabinet now departed and one of the close advisers of the government, which under the title of *The Blair Revolution* tries to define the new tendencies, objectives and directions of the party, largely in terms of a new *style* of government rather than more specifically in regard to its actions, though even some of these are listed. Outside the sphere of direct economic interest there is, for example, the reference to more open government and the need for freedom-of-information legislation. This actually happens to be one of the elements in the Party's programme and election manifesto that has so far not been implemented. There is the election manifesto itself, and this is of considerable importance because election manifestos of a party that has in fact won the election enjoy an important status. Senior civil servants always read election manifestos with great care in order to be prepared for what they might have to deal with if and when this or that party actually wins the election. Moreover, a party that has won the election can usually rely on anything that it does to implement an election manifesto pledge as enjoying a special parliamentary status because it is considered to have received the prior agreement of the electorate and, therefore, even the opposition has to exercise a certain amount of care in opposing its implementation. Then there are certain debates and controversies, newspaper articles from the early days of the new government in which prominent members – Gordon Brown, for example, the Chancellor of the Exchequer – took part with former leading figures of earlier Labour governments, such as Roy (now Lord) Hattersley. Much of this was of a somewhat abstract character and related to such matters as egalitarianism and redistribution aspects of old Labour, which New Labour regarded as not being compelling as far as its policies were concerned.

A particularly detailed and searching analysis of what might be the 'philosophy' of the new Labour government is contained in an article written by a former politician – now academic – who was himself a member of an earlier Labour government, namely David Marquand. This is not the place to go into the detail of his argument because it is primarily of interest to political philosophers and historians of the ups and downs of political parties. The trouble with any analysis of this kind, even so searching a one as I am referring to, is that it is of relatively limited relevance to what governments actually do, to how what they do is actually received by the public and to the effect it has on its future eligibility for office.

A few further words may, however, be said about the broader

political philosophy that seems to inspire the present government. This is more easily done by looking at the aspects of Labour Party policy over a very long period of time that have now been dropped, or are no longer visible in the forefront of the party's programmes, than by looking at what is left of the old, let alone of what has been added that is new to it. The first thing to note, although this to some extent had already taken place before the new government came into power, is that any kind of 'class' image of the Labour Party has since disappeared. The Labour Party today, certainly as represented by the present government, does not stand, and would not wish to be thought of as standing, for any particular section or class of the community. 'The working class' is a phrase that hardly ever appears now in political parlance. The attitude to the trade unions, which is highly controversial at the moment, itself demonstrates even more precisely this difference from the past. The link with the trade unions had been weakening for a long time and while under the present government it has not disappeared, it is now of a very tenuous character. The government has, however, implemented some of its election pledges, particularly in regard to the recognition of trade unions by employers and their place in bargaining, as well as to minimum wage legislation. The government quite explicitly prides itself on being a government for all the people, and it is almost certain that any other kind of attitude would hardly win it much support from the electorate.

In the second place, although previous governments and the Labour Party of earlier decades never explicitly claimed to be anti-business or even anti-capitalist, except on certain 'special' occasions, the present government has gone out of its way to demonstrate its friendly attitude towards business. This takes the form not only of specific declarations to that effect, but also that of close links with important leading members of the business community in industry, trade and finance.

The third aspect, rather less clearly marked by comparison with the past, is a much more tolerant attitude towards the media. The old Labour Party accepted the fact that with very few exceptions indeed the press was not favourably disposed towards it and very often quite hostile. There were exceptions. The *Mirror*, for example, for many years was a Labour-friendly paper, and now and again even other sections of the press showed a certain benevolence towards Labour. Today the government seems unprepared to recognize and accept the certain hostility, or at least broad antagonism, of the major part of the British press. They do not actually acknowledge it and they certainly do not fight it, but on the other hand they try to gain support here and there, most notably from the paper that helped apparently to bring it into power, namely the *Sun*, a member of a group in which there are many papers highly critical, as a rule, of the government.

As far as economics is concerned, the old class-based policy of Labour parties and governments, namely the nationalization of the means of production, distribution and exchange, the celebrated Clause 4, has long since gone. There is no doctrinal remnant of this left in the present government's policy. Where, for example, a minimum of regulation is looked for, accepted and even introduced, this is done not on grounds of political philosophy at all, but on practical grounds of the management of the economy. Where state ownership still exists – a very much narrower segment than it used to be – it usually does so simply because the government has not 'got round' to its privatization.

In regard to broader social questions – 'equality', removal of poverty, providing a safety net for the underprivileged – there is still a good deal of the old attitude left in the present government, but it is not, so to speak, a comprehensive, doctrinal, basis of policy. Indeed the attitude towards the welfare system is distinctly pragmatic and designed to remove, although not explicitly so, the universality that marked the earlier Labour Party attitude towards the provision of minimum standards of living and social security for the population as a whole.

What I have said above may give the impression that this is in some respects a 'do-nothing' government. This is certainly not the case. In many respects the government is justified in claiming, as it has done at the time of its first 'Annual Report' of its stewardship, that it has been a very reforming government. It certainly has done a great deal both in legislation and by other methods in this relatively short time. It certainly has transformed much of the landscape, both economic and in other respects, of the country's activities. What I tried to bring out in what I said above is something different, namely that whatever the government has done, and whatever it appears to be likely to be doing in the future, does not seem to be derived from any perceptible framework of economic, social, political persuasion, not to say ideology. If this is indeed the case, and we shall only know this for certain after more time has gone by, then that would be very much of an innovation, certainly for a Labour Party. Conservative parties in the past, and to a large extent Liberal parties too, have been rather of that kind anyway; but for a Labour Party to be more or less devoid of a philosophical framework is a considerable innovation, whether good or bad I shall try to judge later on.

It may be appropriate at this stage also to say a few words about the general attitude of the new government to Europe and European integration above all. This is a subject that I analysed, including the history of British attitude, in more detail earlier. Here one can say that when the party came into power in 1997, Europe did not play a crucial part in its electoral programme nor in the attitude of the electors that put it into power. It certainly could not be said that its large majority was due either to a greater willingness to go along with European integration, or to a lesser one than had been the case before. Perhaps remarkably, although the issue of Europe was pretty actively debated in the Conservative and in the Labour Parties – not so in the Liberal Democratic Party, which was more or less committed to a forthcoming attitude – it did not seem to play an important part in the election.

When I have said that New Labour is distinguished by not having any of the long-standing traditions and characteristics of the old Labour Party, or indeed of socialist or social democratic parties elsewhere, I did not mean to say that there was no characteristic at all. The party appears to be a broadly 'social-democratic' party, which rejects privilege, for example by its commitment to abolish the hereditary principle in the House of Lords. More generally wealth in itself, or inherited status as such, as justifications for privilege are not acceptable to New Labour and to the present government. It is, therefore, not surprising that it has been argued by many people that it is not significantly different from the Liberal Democratic Party, with which indeed its relationship nowadays is quite close and with which it has worked together in many things. For example, the Electoral Reform Committee that has been set up under Lord Jenkins of Hillhead, a Liberal Democrat, is very largely based on a common purpose of the two parties. It is, however, clear that the resulting proposals have not been entirely to the liking of both of them. Certainly the new Labour Party shows no distinction from the Conservative Party. It is perhaps also appropriate in this context to mention the attempt made by a number of Labour leaders a few years ago to change the character of the then Labour Party, possibly not in a very different direction from that which has emerged under the present Labour leadership, the so-called revolt of the Gang of Four. It was led by Lord Jenkins and included Mr (now Lord) Rogers, Mrs (now Lady) Williams and Dr (now Lord) David Owen. It was an attempt, as it was then put by them, to 'break the mould' of parties and many of the existing political structures and relations. The revolt was short-lived. Many people argued that it was a mistake to create a separate party, and the four innovators or reformers would have done better to stay inside the Labour Party and work for change within the party itself. This is of course an argument that can never be resolved now, and at any event it has ceased to be of relevance since three of the then rebels are now Liberal Democrat peers and one, Dr Owen, who for a time stayed with his own new splinter group, now sits on the cross benches. It is not entirely clear what his political orientation now is, other than that he has become anti-Europe.

Perhaps the most important feature of New Labour's policy that might be mentioned that is not immediately and directly relevant to its economic programme is the great emphasis placed upon education. Again and again the leaders speak of it and emphasize the great importance they attach to it and the changes they wish to bring about to ensure a much more adequate training and education system for the British people, including fulfilling the purpose of making it appropriate for the new millennium. The Liberal Democrats of course not only support this but from time to time claim to want to do even more than the government. As for the Tories, they do not dissent from it either and their criticism is mainly of a more detailed character, attacking the methods and the allocation of funds and so on, rather than the very principle of having a more substantial and a more effective educational system.

There is little doubt that the present educational system in our country – primary, secondary and higher education as well as all the various technical branches of education and its relationship to scientific research, adult education and so on – is in a fairly chaotic state and that much needs to be done to put it right. What exactly this should be is of course not an appropriate subject for this book, but if in fact the Labour government, despite the pressures of day-to-day requirements in the economic and political field, including foreign affairs, as well as a crowded legislative programme, can at the end of five or ten years have achieved an educational system that will command the respect and admiration of a substantial part of the population and of other nations, that will indeed be an enormous achievement, and any failures in other respects would pale into insignificance.

Next to education the other great national activity of the state that the Labour government has stressed is health. This again is a very specialized subject and the reforms made in recent years by successive governments, particularly by Tory governments, have not produced a health system that is effective and commands universal respect and approval. What is perhaps on a minor level worth noticing is that the emphasis on education and health has the virtue of separating these two largest areas of public expenditure from what is called welfare. Education and health must be regarded more as in the nature of investment in the infrastructure of the population than as welfare, although it is not easy to keep the two distinct, especially as regards health care. But in fact it is really important from the point of view of the true appreciation of the financial consequences of what the State either does directly or causes to be done by private agencies of one kind or another in these areas. They should not be lumped together with welfare in the strict sense of the word.

Care for old age – that is to say a pension system – requires rather more careful delineation from welfare, i.e. help to the underprivileged, who for one reason or another require support from the state. Here again successive governments have tried to produce a system that would emphasize the insurance aspect of pensions. This could make it more self-sustaining and reduce the need for state support. However, assistance from public funds could still be needed where otherwise provision would be inadequate for what is regarded as a proper level of old-age standards in a civilized and advanced society. The government has in fact produced new pension proposals and it remains to be seen how these will be received and implemented.

It might be said at this stage that to some extent the argument about welfare and the future of the welfare state so-called is clouded by the very word 'welfare'. This has a certain eleemosynary connotation and therefore tends to prevent a careful distinction between different types of benefit.

Although the political parties themselves may consider that their plans and attitudes in regard to, say, education, health, pensions and welfare in the strictest sense of the word, are very different, in fact the aspects that divide the parties are very different from those that existed not so very many years ago. Certainly, as far as the Labour Party is concerned, as I have already indicated, a Labour Party without any kind of ideological echo at least of its past, seems almost a contradiction in terms. However, this is not to say that, from a strictly political point of view in the sense of gaining and maintaining power, it is wrong or ineffective. Certainly what seems to have been a major factor in 1997 in the amazing victory of the party is that it did carry with it a certain atmosphere of innovation and change, which responded to some feeling in the electorate.

Of the many tenets of political philosophy that have from time to time characterized Labour, egalitarianism in one form or another has probably been the most constant. It certainly formed a major subject of controversy between the 'Old Guard' and 'New Labour', or some of its leaders at any rate, immediately after the election. At that time, as I have already mentioned, the leadership was regarded as showing a lack of enthusiasm for egalitarianism and this was largely defended by those accused on the ground that in present-day society the important thing was equal opportunity rather than equal outcome. However, it is by no means certain that the present government, despite a certain reluctance to pronounce new, broad political principles, let alone echo old ones, has totally given up any question of redistributive fiscal policy. Certainly it would be no less anxious than the other political parties to be able at some point to reduce the basic rate of income tax. That would obviously be a very popular political move and at the same time could have a degree of redistributive effect. As far as other forms of personal taxation are concerned, for instance capital gains tax on individuals or inheritance tax, the Labour government has not as yet indicated any particular objectives but may well without any kind of doctrinal commitment produce some amelioration. In this connection it is interesting to note that it was reported that one of the leaders of the Conservative Party had hoped during the last government to produce major reductions in both these taxes. As far as indirect taxation is concerned, here also a measure of redistribution is almost inevitable and has to some degree already taken place, particularly in regard to VAT. Whether the government will be able to escape altogether some involvement in certain aspects of incomes policy, despite the fact that the experiments in this direction of earlier Labour governments are far from encouraging, remains to be seen. This applies for example to the high level of executive salaries in the City and elsewhere, which sometimes reach bizarre, not to say obscene levels, and which are particularly striking in the case of the emoluments paid to the managements of newly privatized utilities. These certainly have already attracted the attention of some of the members of the government and have led to demands for restraint similar to what the government has been urging in relation to wage claims in the private sector. What the result of all this will be we shall try to examine again a bit further on, but they are certainly areas that, if not directly within the field of broad political philosophy, nevertheless do have a substantial relationship to it and awaken substantial echoes of older debates within the Labour movement.

It is not excluded that out of the great emphasis on education and training, the reform of the welfare system and the creation of equal opportunity by whatever means are still open to the government both in legislation and through what the Americans call 'jaw-boning', some kind of broad political-philosophical framework for New Labour may emerge. This might well not matter all that much from a narrow political point of view in gaining and keeping power, but might satisfy the more intellectual demands of some of their followers.

This excursion into more theoretical aspects of political philosophy as far as they affect the new Labour government is meant to be a kind of bridge between the account of what appear to be the requirements of the British economy over the next ten to twenty years and an examination, in so far as it is already possible to make it, of which way the present government for a major part of this period is likely to lead the country. We may return to it at the end of our study as a kind of summing-up of this examination of New Labour.

On the other side there is the question of macro-economic policy in its monetary aspects. Here the government is also being criticized by some, and this is much less justifiable in my view, not only on the ground of pursuing a rigorous anti-inflation policy, but also of having entrusted the use of the main instrument to this end, namely control of short-term interest rates, to the Central Bank rather than maintaining direct control of the Treasury. I think there is a general acceptance that the maintenance of a strict anti-inflationary policy is not only highly desirable in itself, but is to a large extent a condition for creating a better atmosphere for business enterprise and indeed for many of the social reforms that the government has in mind. One of the problems is that the anti-inflationary policy has over a whole period of time now gradually been concentrated on one instrument only, namely that of monetary policy, and the trouble with that instrument is that it is not only not always very precise in its effects, but that it does tend to have rather difficult side effects. These relate primarily to the exchange rate and it is generally accepted not only that significant fluctuations in exchange rates are undesirable, but that some of the ones that are brought about by monetary policy justified on the grounds of anti-inflation have, because of their effect on exports and therefore on industry generally, very unpleasant consequences.

The remedy in the opinion of some people, including myself, lies in finding a regime in which the exchange rate could be isolated to a large extent from the consequences of monetary policy and in closely co-ordinating monetary policy itself with a suitable fiscal policy. I deal more fully with the problem of monetary policy below.

The question that arises is the government's attitude to the European Union, and more particularly to the creation of Economic and Monetary Union. On this the present government has shown both before the election and since a greater benevolence to Europe. However, these friendly gestures have, as I have said, not yet extended to any very definite statement concerning the government's intentions about EMU. Indeed the government is committed to a referendum before it can actually join and, therefore, has acted in stating that it cannot join the first wave. I should perhaps also add that this is regrettable. It is no less clear than it has been now for a number of years, not only in regard to EMU itself, although this happens to be the most immediate and pressing point on the political agenda of Europe, but more generally, that the British role has not done it very much good despite the hype that has surrounded our recent economic performance compared with that of some other countries. It is, I think, still clear that a good deal of the remedy for some of the dilemmas in which our policy, monetary and fiscal, has landed us, could be mitigated, if not altogether resolved, by closer participation in European integration, including above all membership in EMU. However, on all this, as on so much that concerns the actions of the present government, I will say more later.

More generally on international policy, the attitude of the government is so far not substantially different from that of its predecessors. Nor is it easy to say how it could differ very much from it. Relations with the United States have of course continued, and must continue, to be close and friendly and there seems to be a certain amount of rapport between the government leadership and the White House. As regards Central and Eastern Europe, the government is not in a position to play a very different role from that of other major countries, including particularly other Western European countries, and indeed in some respects cannot even be as active as, say, Germany. More generally, the government has indicated a disposition to let ethical considerations have more of an impact on the fashioning of foreign policy than they had before. This applies to such matters, for example, as trade in arms with certain countries where there is a general feeling of lack of respect for human rights, or other matters that offend the general sense of proper conduct in international affairs. How far the government will be able to reconcile these considerations with the inherited and long-standing economic interest in some of these regards, both as concerns the countries involved and the type of trade, including arms, it is not yet easy to see.

It will be interesting to observe – and at the moment there are no very clear indications – how the government's relations with China develop now that the Hong Kong problem has disappeared from the immediate agenda. There should be no difficulty – indeed there probably would not have been with a government of a different political colour – in developing friendly and fruitful relations with the People's Republic of China, which is still, as I have already indicated earlier, on a path of rapid industrial and general economic development, including in the financial field, liberalization and increasing trade and other relations with the outside world.

As far as the government's relations with business – that is to say both industry and finance – are concerned, so far at least they have continued to be as friendly as the party's pre-election stance indicated. The government has introduced a number of reforms and has availed itself of the help of prominent businessmen, including in ministerial office.

The government has introduced a number of reforms in the financial field, including a new system of supervision of financial services, the precise effect of which is not yet clear. It will be based largely on the old Securities and Investment Board, to which a new head has been appointed – the former Deputy Governor of the Bank of England. It will have a structure not yet entirely defined, ensuring the supervision of all, or practically all, the different financial services that have hitherto been looked after by separate supervisory agencies. The government is shortly to publish a bill to set up the new Financial Services Authority and it may go through parliament in this session. The supervision of the banks themselves has been moved from the Bank of England to this new body. This has not been welcomed by the Bank, though it is not clear whether it was the decision or the manner in which it was taken that caused offence. It is difficult to see how with the reform that is now being instituted the supervision of banks could have been left unchanged. However, it is to be expected that the experience that the Bank of England has in these matters will be fully taken over by the new body and also that close relations with the Bank will continue to exist. The reason for this is that in the exercise of monetary policy it is essential that the operating authority, i.e. the Bank of England, should be in a position to acquire all the knowledge it can about the status and activity of the various parts of the financial services industry, which by their activities have an influence on the total sphere over which monetary policy has to be exercised.

On the broader domestic front, the government appears to have a very heavy programme in mind. The list of 'reviews' and the indications of future reforms include a number of substantial changes in the general framework that I have already mentioned, such as criminal justice.

Of the longer-term, broader issues, I have mentioned electoral reform. In this area there are all sorts of practical issues involved, and here again it is hardly to be expected that given all the other things the government has to contend with at the moment, it will be a matter of urgent priority except possibly in regard to elections of the European Parliament.

Of greater and of more immediate significance is devolution, that is to say a greater degree of self-government for Wales and an even greater one for Scotland, where the creation of a separate Scottish Parliament, including some taxing powers, has happened. The changes have been decided by referenda, which certainly have an immediate beneficial effect on the record of the government whatever their long-term consequences for the structure of the United Kingdom, for England and possibly more for the future of Northern Ireland.

A framework for a solution to the problems of Northern Ireland that could last some time has been created. However, at the moment of writing violence is still threatening.

I mention these matters not because they fit very readily into the framework of what I have been discussing so far about the development of the last few decades, but because they are matters that by all appearances under the present government may become more actively debated and perhaps even decided over the next two parliaments. They are not matters that directly affect the issues I have discussed, and it remains to be seen whether, if and when put into practice, they have a direct bearing on economic policy and on politics in the narrower sense of the word as I have described it so far.

In analysing and assessing the story so far told of the three generations of recent British economic and political development – not in detail but in its broad outline – it cannot be possible as yet to take into account anything that the new government may promise and may perform on these broader matters. We must therefore proceed, as I propose to do in the next sections, to such an analysis and assessment, allowing, where possible, for any indications from current policy decisions and tendencies. It is unlikely that it will be possible to decide now whether the future chronicler will be able to say about 1 May 1997, 'Bliss was it in that dawn to be alive.'

The Course of the Economy

Even on a simple extrapolation of what has happened during the last two decades it is easy to see that the next twenty years will produce very great changes in the way in which the economy behaves. These will be due primarily to changes outside the economic framework itself, and certainly to a large extent separate from any brought about by deliberate economic policy by the authorities. We can already see that what has been put in train recently in regard to many of the major activities will go on changing. This is true of a number of industries – telecommunications, information technology, travel (particularly air travel) – and also of modes of living, housing, tourism and the whole structure of the ways in which people, at any rate in large urban conglomerations, procure their daily needs.

Many of these changes have been started and will continue as a result of their own dynamism. This is certainly true of those that have been brought about by technology, which, in turn, derive from changes in basic scientific advance. This is also true of health care where, as I have already mentioned in a different context, the ability to deal with disease either by surgical procedures or by the use of compounds and the new techniques of caring for the sick will go on developing possibly even faster than hitherto.

Many changes have been brought about by changes of policy, particularly by the great wave of liberalization and the disappearance of many restrictive practices and regulations either by governments or by organized sections of the community, which has been a hallmark of the last twenty years or so. Just to take one example, the competitive forces released in the air travel industry or in telecommunications have brought about a complete revolution in the way in which people can now use the facilities available to them in both these industries. And this will certainly go on.

But this is not what I am primarily concerned with here. What we want to know is how the economy will alter – that is to say the sum total of what has so often been described in text books as 'men in the ordinary business of life' – while these changes are going on over the next twenty years. For a start, it might be as well to look at what would be the desirable objectives of economic development over this period. Then we can consider how many of these are likely to emerge 'spontaneously', that is, without any direct intervention or at least any major intervention on the part of organized society. We can then consider what role 'authority', i.e. organized intervention, particularly by government, can play in modifying the result for the better.

As the first desirable objective of economic development one can say that it would be as well if the economy was not subject to violent fluctuations over the next two decades, but developed in as steady a manner as possible. This is a little different from what has become fashionably called the acceptance or the rejection of 'boom and bust'. From the point of view of political controversy, particularly in qualifying what earlier governments have done and what later governments wish and claim to do, the distinction between a steady economy and one that is subject to boom and bust is a convenient way of making political capital. But if by absence of boom and bust it is meant that the economy is not subject to any fluctuations whatsoever, this is out of the question. Neither historical record, nor theoretical analysis of the way in which the economy behaves will make this plausible. For one thing, investment clearly is discontinuous in the sense that it takes place by 'quanta' over time. It cannot be stopped, reversed, annulled or changed without any time lag whatsoever, and there-fore presumably without any effect on people involved in the establishment of this investment and in its change over time.

So some fluctuation must be expected and if the external factors, such as technological developments, are of a very revol-utionary and sudden character, then sometimes the ups and downs of the economy that are consequent upon these changes will be quite considerable. But it is clearly in the interests of ordinary human beings, who are both the agents of the economy as well as its objects and sometimes its victims, that these fluctuations should as far as possible not be unduly violent. We shall see later whether it is possible to bring this about and how it might be done. Some fluctuations are brought about by policy and policy changes and we shall need to consider how these can be avoided or minimized.

The other objectives are much more specific. Growth is the first one of these. An adequate level of growth is clearly highly desirable, and indeed essential if the changes that are about to take place in the surrounding environment are to be properly accommodated and if the aspirations of mankind, which are notoriously unlimited as far as economic goods and services are concerned, are to be satisfied. It is not easy to set a particular target, but a growth per annum over the period of twenty years of around a figure of 2.5 per cent would obviously be highly desirable. The need for growth ought perhaps to be more closely identified. As I have said, human aspirations are one factor; the other is demographic. It is true that in our country, as is indeed the case in many other highly industrialized countries of the West, the rate of population growth has greatly abated and occasionally even looks like becoming stationary. Nevertheless, change is taking place. The age structure of the population changes and with it growth of the economy becomes necessary because the needs of the different age classes of the population differ. Certainly the new, younger generations are not going to be satisfied without reaping the benefit of whatever technological and other changes make possible for the satisfaction of human wants. So a degree of growth is essential. Technological unemployment (which according to the eminent economist Wassily Leontief will continue and increase) presents another reason for aiming at economic growth, particularly in the provision of services.

To enjoy growth, however, requires a number of other things to take place. It requires first of all that if growth is to take place, the workforce, given the changes which will inevitably occur in the character, substance and method of industrial and economic activity, should be made adaptable and capable of coping with these changes. And that means a very substantial degree of continuous training, not only training for specific jobs, but training in the wider sense (including what is better called education) so as to create a readiness for adaptation and for switching from certain types of activity to others swiftly and without pain. This does not necessarily mean accepting completely any particular theory of the transferability of talent and of physical and mental abilities. Nevertheless, there is something in the broader training for adaptation that must go hand in hand with the rather more difficult to identify adaptability for specific new tasks that may come along.

Again, if growth is also to mean better living standards, then necessarily labour policy, which means policy in regard to wages and remuneration generally at all levels of economic activity, as well as hours of work in relation to hours of leisure, should be properly adapted and remain adaptable to changing economic circumstances.

Much of what I have stipulated about growth and the enjoyment of the fruits of growth could be expected to come along, so to speak, spontaneously, that is to say really as a development of the dynamic of the economic process itself. We have already seen a great deal of this happening; for example, changes in work habits and in the composition of the workforce, the degree to which part-time as against full-time employment has developed. The use of female labour is perhaps the most striking of these; indeed the status and position of women in society, and more particularly in the economy, has changed out of all recognition. This is perhaps in many ways the most striking development of recent years. Again, there is a significant development of work from home rather than work from an office or a factory, even if this no longer corresponds to William Blake's 'dark satanic mills'. It is more than likely that the development of information technology and telecommunications will increase the extent to which much of the more technical and less physical type of economic activity

74

may be carried on from home rather than from a specific work-place. There are of course social factors also at work here. I have already mentioned the increased employment of women. This is changing the old structure of family life, which is contributing, and will contribute, towards the disappearance of much of what are regarded as the proper spheres of activity of the man and the woman within the family. It would no longer be the universal pattern that the man goes out to his factory or to his office while the wife stays at home either looking after the children or doing housework. All this is already changing in some societies, for instance in the Scandinavian ones, and I am sure will also change in our own.

However, all these inherent changes of the economy's own dynamic do not necessarily guarantee that the fruits of economic growth will be readily available for absorption by economic agents, as they are nowadays called, let alone that they will be distributed in a way that will keep society in a reasonable state of cohesion and harmony. It is at this point that we must look at how far intervention in the process of technological change, economic growth and the ordering of the economy by the social institutions, particularly by central government and its various agencies, monetary and otherwise, can be influenced so as to make a satisfactory development more certain than it otherwise would be. In looking at this part of the problem, it is as well to emphasize once again that the social institutions that we have created and that are in themselves changing all the time, particularly central government, are far from omniscient, let alone omnipotent: they do not necessarily know what it is that would best contribute towards the most desirable economic development and they certainly do not have at their disposal all the necessary instruments that would make it possible for them to bring a desirable development about, even if they could clearly identify it. However, although government may be a 'poor thing', it is the only thing we have got to intervene in the economic process and to create order where otherwise there is always a danger of a lapse into anarchy either social or political, and certainly economic.

Acquiring an adequate knowledge of where the economy is and where it is going and what it is desirable to do either in the way of letting it move the way it is moving or changing the direction must of course come first. On the face of it, here the developments over recent decades, and indeed over the last two centuries, have been startling in the extreme. But it is by no means certain that they have necessarily been totally effective. We now have, compared, say, even to the thirties, an apparatus of data-gathering and organizing and displaying statistics, and various forms of forecasting likely future developments from the existing body of statistics, which are quite staggering in their complexity and in their claims for accuracy and effectiveness. It is within my recollection, and no doubt that of many others, that only some years ago Harold Macmillan complained bitterly that he had to run the economy as if he were running a railroad on 'last year's timetable'. Indeed others were complaining at the same time that it was impossible to forecast the future when you did not even have an accurate picture of where you were at the moment. Certainly the self-confidence of statisticians and forecasters has grown a great deal. How far that self-confidence is justified is a pretty contentious matter and very often, given the normal conduct of political debate in our country, a matter of quite fierce argument between different political parties and between those who are in government and those who are not and hope to be at another time.

Without accepting the more extreme formulations of the forecaster's art – and art it is, not science – it would be wrong to reject altogether what has been developed in this area of statistical assessment of the situation and attempts to project its development into the future. However, caution is essential. In particular it does not at all follow that the near future is easier to forecast than the more distant future. In some cases it is, in others not. Indeed in some cases it is easier to be reasonably certain as to where we shall be a year or two from now than to be quite certain where we shall be in six months' time.

Inevitably the success of the forecaster is to a large extent tied to the theoretical framework within which he is trying to organize, and deduce from, a series of actual data – in other words, from the sort of model that he uses for his purpose. Model-building has became a growth industry in the last fifty years or so. It was in its infancy before the War, but has grown greatly since the end of the War. Leaving aside the more technical aspects of different models, with which it is not either necessary nor possible to deal here, most of them derive from relatively few basic theoretical concepts. These are usually traceable to some of the more innovative and inventive economists of the last fifty years, particularly Keynes, from whom much of the model-building of a certain type is derived. Inevitably, therefore, in so far as the quantitative deductions based on some particular model are traceable to a more theoretical, not to say ideological, background, they will bear the birthmarks of that background and will appeal to different types of recipients of the resulting forecast, depending upon which ideological framework they prefer. It is not possible to draw up, as it were, a systematic catalogue of these varieties and we must, therefore, of necessity make do with forecasts as they emerge from the practitioners of this art. Inevitably, particularly when it comes to more specific forecasts, such as movements in foreign exchange rates or movements in stock markets, the public (which is to be divided between the broad general public and the professional market operators) will tend to rely most on those whose guesses have been more correct in the past. This may not be highly satisfactory from a scientific point of view, but there is very little else that is available.

Apart from relying on forecasts produced by professionals from various sentiments of one kind or another about the state of the economy and its future course, from lobbyists, and from political reports, which come to ministers from various sources both within and outside their own political ken, the authorities form some kind of a picture upon which they can then base whatever action they take.

It is at this point that one must look at what actual instruments are available to them for acting in one way or another on the mass of information that they have got, ranging from specific forecasts to reports from party agents in the constituencies or casual remarks made by businessmen whom they meet at dinner parties, and so on.

Broadly speaking these instruments fall into three classes: (a) the heavy artillery, so to speak, of legislation, which must be mainly designed for major and more long-term lasting changes of an economic character; (b) fiscal changes, i.e. the manipulation of the public finances through the budget both in its annual guise and by occasional intermediate changes in 'getting and spending'; and (c) monetary changes, which in recent years have acquired a particularly important status both in public and in the actual exercise of governmental power.

I have referred to legislation as the heavy artillery, and that indeed it is. A great many changes that governments wish to introduce – reforms of earlier policy or entirely new areas that require statutory backing before they can become part of practice in the economic field – do require legislation. Governments get elected usually on a manifesto, which may or may not be very detailed and contain specific pledges. But where it does contain them, and where these require legislation for their implementation, this becomes a very special feature of a government's programme. They enjoy special status and indeed one might say even a special respect in their parliamentary passage. An opposition that saw a government elected with an adequate majority would be very careful indeed before it really tried to obstruct the passage of legislation that was designed to give effect to a pledge that the government had made in its manifesto. Manifestos of course are also studied extremely carefully before the election by the higher Civil Service as an indication of what they might have to cope with if this or that party got elected and they had then to put into effect some, if not all, of the provisions of their election manifesto.

I shall revert to this later, but even now one can give examples over a very wide field of economic and financial problems that have already been the subject of legislation in this new government at the time of writing. For example, there is the Bank of England Act, of which the most important provision is the creation of a Monetary Policy Committee that gives effect to the Chancellor's decision to make the Bank of England operationally independent in determining short-term interest rates. At the other extreme we have the Minimum Wages Act, which for the first time in our recent history gives effect to the government's pledge to create a minimum wage. What it actually has done has not met by any means with the wholehearted approval of the trade unions, who have been pressing for such legislation for a long time. If the government were to follow some of its Continental neighbours in introducing new limits to the working week, that would also have to be enshrined in legislation and passed by parliament.

Fiscal measures are by nature part of the legislative programme of the government because of the traditional annual budget, which has become a sort of regular ritual in the government's economic timetable.

The management of the finances of the sovereign, later of the democratic, state has always been recognized as a potent instrument in determining the fate of the economy as a whole because, even at its most sparing, the budget does take out a significant proportion of the gross product of the nation and spends it for purposes of its own, but which naturally also affect the average citizen. For a long time that was how the annual budget, that is to say the disposition of the government's taxing and spending powers, was regarded. Adam Smith, whose *Wealth of Nations* sets out inter alia the correct canons of taxation, thought that the management of the state's household was in principle no different from that of the household of a single family. For a long time that was indeed how fiscal policy was looked upon, and sound finance, as far as the public was concerned, was explicitly, or implicitly at least, likened to that which a prudent householder would do with his own resources in his own income and spending patterns.

The major revolution that Keynes introduced, but which had been brewing for a long time before, and which is not as often recognized as one of his major changes as some of his other

contributions to economic science, was to break with that tradition. Keynes in fact demonstrated that what the state did by
taxing and spending was different from what an individual or
single company did with its own income and its own expenditure.
Because the size of the finance managed by the state, the proportion of the nation's product that it took and disposed of as it
decided, admittedly under parliamentary control, determined to
a very large extent the course of the economy, it was therefore
totally different. Even those who do not follow Keynes in many
of his other doctrines admit that this was obviously a major change
and controversies about what is to be the right fiscal policy today
do not turn so much on the actual narrower accounting of getting
and spending, but rather on the wider economic impact of the
State's management of its own finances.

The third of the instruments of policy available to the government is monetary policy. This has lately taken on a very special
meaning because of the decision by the present Chancellor to
entrust the Bank of England, through its Monetary Policy Committee, with the powers of fixing short-term interest rates. It now
does this once a month. The committee consists of nine members
and is charged with the duty of maintaining stable prices as
defined by an inflation target set by the Chancellor.

Monetary Policy

'Let no one suppose that monetary policy is an easy option. I do not mean by this that a strict monetary policy is difficult to effect, true though that is. But one must realize that monetary policy involves very serious economic consequences before one can hope that inflation will be contained by it.

'A strict monetary policy means rising interest rates and less credit. Any hope that it might be possible to keep a tight hold on the money supply – to quote the fashionable phrase – without accepting the implication for interest rates, is illusory, since it is just through changes in the relative rates of return on assets, real as well as financial, that monetary policy works. The higher cost and the lessened availability of funds will make capital expenditures by companies, both for fixed investment and for stockbuilding, seem less worthwhile. I realize that the disincentive effect of rising interest rates is lessened if the rate of price inflation is seen to be rising at the same time. Nevertheless, if monetary pressure goes on mounting, then the point must come when general business confidence is affected; and once expectations start being revised, the direction of the economy can be very quickly altered.

'When real demand begins to grow by less than productive potential, unemployment results. The rise in unemployment, and the concurrent development of buyers' markets, should help to reduce inflation, though current developments here and abroad have not made me confident that one could forecast what extent or what duration of unemployment might be necessary to achieve this purpose. But if the aim of a tight monetary policy is to cure inflation by means of raising unemployment, one would want to ask whether there are not better ways of curing inflation than by purposely wasting resources, particularly at a time of low growth;

and even if it were argued that a much larger margin of unemployment was a necessary evil – which I do not – would it really make sense to achieve this degree of deflation by placing the main reliance on monetary measures?

'Some people seem to think that monetary policy could be used to counter inflation without involving this traumatic development. They hope that monetary pressure would act directly upon employers to make them less prepared to meet inflationary wage claims, and that thereby one could get a general decline in monetary expansion, wages and prices simultaneously without any necessary increase in unemployment. This seems to me to be oversimplified. The outcome of wage negotiation depends on a lot of factors, and it is not clear why the impact of monetary pressures should change the balance of bargaining power between unions and employers directly. It will do so indirectly if monetary pressures weaken the markets for the industrialist's goods sufficiently, so that he is likely to face greater difficulty in passing on wage increases in higher prices. But this brings us right back to using monetary restriction to cut expenditures, and, subsequently, to increasing unemployment. Indeed, it is this threat of unemployment to the worker, as well as the implication of lower profit margins to the industrialist, that in theory at least finally makes the policy bite upon wage negotiations. It is, I suppose, possible to imagine that the adoption of a more restrictive monetary policy could so change expectations about future prospects for inflation and for the markets for labour and for goods that inflationary wage settlements would subside spontaneously, as it were, without much increase in unemployment having to occur. All I can say is that those who believe that will believe anything, so long as it has a happy ending.'

I have inserted the above paragraphs inside inverted commas because they are in fact an extract from a lecture that I gave in 1970 on a subject that is of very considerable importance and much debated nowadays. I felt it appropriate to insert it in my present disquisition on monetary policy as one of the instruments of macro-economic management.

If I had to write these paragraphs today, no doubt the formulation and the use of this phrase or that might be a little different because the current vocabulary in which these matters are discussed is somewhat different from what it was. But I do not think that I would wish to change the nature of the argument itself from what I thought to write twenty-eight years ago in circumstances that had some similarity to the present ones, although they were by no means as far-reaching in their consequence as they now are. The actual debate, particularly political debate, on monetary matters and monetary policy became even more acute a few years after I had written the above with the advent of a Conservative government under Mrs Thatcher in which monetarism, so-called, was supposed to triumph and monetary policy be the main, perhaps even the exclusive, instrument of macro-economic management.

Today, the debate on what monetary policy should be, what its consequences are, which are the good ones and which are the more doubtful ones, centres, in our country at least, primarily on the activities of the Monetary Policy Committee of the Bank of England, the Bank having been given independence – at any rate operational independence, as it was named – by the present government, and indeed this is enshrined in the Bank of England Act, one of the earliest bits of legislation in economic matters passed by the present parliament.

The debate about the activities of the Monetary Policy Committee comprises a number of aspects. One of them turns on whether the Bank of England, through its Monetary Policy Committee, should indeed have operational independence. On this point I have no doubt that the decision of the government was right. An independent panel, which I chaired some two or three years ago before the government came into power, did in fact recommend a system of independence with accountability, which is in most respects exactly what the government has in fact installed. I do not think that the problems connected with finding the right monetary policy, either per se or in connection with other aspects of economic policy, is significantly affected by whether it is done under the present system – that is to say with the government setting targets and defining the way in which these targets should be measured, but leaving the execution of policy to reach these targets to another agency – or whether this is all combined in the breast, so to speak, of the Chancellor of the Exchequer. Indeed, one of the arguments for separating these functions is that the possibility of an intrusion to an undesirable extent of 'political' considerations is avoided by making the Central Bank the executant of monetary policy.

Another aspect that is often criticized, and inevitably so, is whether the actual decisions of the Monetary Policy Committee of the Bank of England have been correct – in other words, whether the short-term rate of interest that they fixed was put at too high or at too low a level for what was required by the economic situation. This is of course inevitable and again I do not think that it goes to the heart of the problem. I have some sympathy with those who have been arguing that on the whole the monetary policy has been too much moved by fear of inflationary pressures and in consequence has kept short-term interest rates higher than they needed to be, with the consequence that the exchange rate of the pound has been kept at too high a level. The effect on exchange rates has always been notable. Indeed this was true even in the old Gold Standard days, although very often in that system the relationship of cause and effect was a different one. It was the outflow of gold that was either due to, or the cause of, changes in exchange rates, which prompted changes in interest rates so as to reverse the original movement. But today the movement of short-term funds across national boundaries is of enormous magnitude. It is highly sensitive to movement that offers gains in this capital or that. The result is of course very quickly reflected in changes in exchange rates.

This has had the consequence of hurting our export trades and with it manufacturing generally. Manufacturing industry has suffered for other reasons (such as, the Prime Minister has rightly said, the absence of adequate numbers of absolutely first-class managers and so on) and has shrunk considerably in recent years as compared with services as a constituent of the gross domestic product.

I think, however, that the most important flaw, or at least defect, of monetary policy is excessive reliance on movements of short-term interest rates possibly to the exclusion of other policy decisions as an instrument for managing the economy.

There is also much debate on how monetary policy is to be executed. First of all, there are considerable differences of opinion, not only among theoretical economists, but among central bankers, as to how exactly a monetary policy should be executed in so far as it aims, as it usually does, to ensure price stability, i.e. about the avoidance of either inflationary or deflationary movements originating from the side of money. The difference of view turns on whether the target that is chosen for monetary policy should be the symptoms of inflationary (or deflationary) tendencies, primarily as revealed by price indices, or whether it should be the aggregate volume and velocity of circulation of money and credit. This is usually called inflation targeting versus monetary targeting. The latter is said to be practised primarily by the Bundesbank, while the former is almost a sole prerogative of British monetary policy. The difficulty is that both can be criticized as being not perfect indicators of the direction in which monetary policy should go. Inflation targeting is not only subject to difficulties of statistical measurement, but even where these can be overcome, it is always a matter of some speculation whether the trends are clear enough up or down, for example in terms of wage settlements. Is it settlements that should be considered, or is it actual movements in wages, and not only wage rates but actual wage payments that should be the criteria? Furthermore, it is quite clear that the determination of wages is not a uniform phenomenon. For example, it varies particularly markedly as between the public sector, i.e. where the state itself is the employer, and the private sector. Obviously, if the government feels that it is necessary to put a brake on possible inflationary pressures coming from the wage side, they are in a far better position to ensure that this happens to the wages of its own employees rather than having to rely on the private sector with all the variety of bargaining between workers and employers, collectively or not, which often produces quite different results. Indeed, in our own country one of the problems in the recent past has been that while the wages in the state sector have, rightly or wrongly – particularly where teachers, health service workers and so on are concerned – been kept down more or less 'adequately' from the point of view of what are considered to be the right levels in order to avoid inflation, while those in the private sector have risen considerably more.

This is the prime difficulty on the inflation targeting side. I have picked out the question of wage settlements as one. There are many others, particularly the influence of export and import prices, which in turn are dependent on the effect that monetary policy itself has on the exchange rate.

The difficulty with monetary targeting is that here again it is not at all easy to decide which are the critical levels to watch. Measuring the volume of money and credit is in any event not easy, and there have been over the years, particularly during the monetarist phase of governmental policy in our country, a number of different indicators – M_1, M_2, M_3, M_4 and so on, each measuring in a different way what is supposed to be the amount of money and credit that is effectively operating on the price level. I would like to quote an anecdote concerning a man I consider to be probably the wisest of the Governors of the Bank of Japan in recent years – now dead – when I asked him, 'What do you think of M_4?' (which was then the fashion in our country). He thought for a while and then he said: 'You see, I am not quite sure that I understand what M_4 is, and even if I did know how M_4 is defined, I wouldn't quite know what level it ought to have; and even if I knew what level it ought to have, I wouldn't quite know how to measure it; and even if I knew how to measure it, I wouldn't quite know how I could actually reach that particular level. So I don't think much about M_4.'

This is perhaps an extreme view, but it does illustrate the difficulty of monetary targeting. The net result of all this seems to be that it is not at all clear that either inflation targeting or monetary targeting can be totally relied upon. Indeed some of the best results seem to have been achieved by monetary authorities that take both into account, inflationary or deflationary pressures as the case may be, plus actual movements in monetary aggregates as a sort of further test. However, in the outcome one must simply content oneself by recognizing that either way, or a combination of both, cannot be guaranteed to produce first-rate results.

But when all that is said, there remains a further extremely difficult aspect of monetary policy. I referred to it in the paragraphs earlier on in which I quoted from my lecture twenty-eight years ago. What it amounts to basically is that even where monetary policy can be successful (though at a cost, and as I have said at a cost in terms of unemployment, which is not that easy to justify – I shall come back to that in a moment), it is not at all clear that movements in short-term interest rates can hit any particular objective in the absence of many other factors, notably fiscal policy. It is therefore essential to aim at a combination of fiscal and monetary policy, but how this can be achieved and what it would produce if it was achieved, is not easily determined.

What remains certain is that monetary policy by itself can only really reach a particular target, and it is not always certain that the target is the most important one. As I have indicated earlier, the level of foreign exchange rates for the currency in question is probably the most certain target that short-term interest rates can hit and that is not necessarily always the one that is decisive from the point of view of the broader objective of stable prices, which we can readily accept as a very important objective of economic policy.

As regards the question of the cost of monetary policy as the principal instrument and whether the price to be paid in terms of unemployment is right or wrong, I might perhaps add a further point that has become rather more fashionable in debate on this whole subject in our country recently. The Monetary Policy Committee has recognized that there is a relationship between movements of interest rates – particularly if certain levels are maintained for a certain length of time – and the level of employment, and perhaps also economic growth. In this connection much has been made of a relatively modern concept in economic discussion, namely the NAIRU, the non-accelerating inflation rate of unemployment. It is debatable how valuable, and indeed valid, this theoretical concept of a rate of unemployment that would equate with a rate of inflation that does not accelerate really is. But even if this concept has validity and can be used in actual examination of economic developments, what is somewhat surprising is that it has been equated with a 'natural rate of unemployment'. Whether the word 'natural' should appear at all in modern economic discussion is debatable. It was not unknown among earlier economists; it carries with it a certain, shall I say, sanctification of whatever it is applied to that is, in my view, inappropriate in the social sciences. It may have its uses in the natural sciences with their far more exact terminology, but I think in economics, or in any part of the social sciences, it is an extremely dangerous word to use and certainly it should not be applied to the NAIRU of which I spoke earlier.

To conclude this section, one more word about Keynes. I have already mentioned what I regard as the major and fundamental contribution that Keynes made apart from the many more specific ones that are usually described and analysed. This is to put a different complexion on the role of the State's own finances in determining the course of the economy. This new emphasis has given rise to the whole concept and theory of macro-economics and macro-economic policy to which much of what I have said about the instruments available to the State has already been devoted.

I think I should add that the emphasis introduced into economic reasoning by Keynes is by no means to be regarded as leaning in one particular direction of policy or another. For one thing, as I have already mentioned, I do not think that it neces-sarily leads to a *dirigiste* approach, that is to say to an in-built preference for state intervention and state action rather than to the absence thereof. Nor is it, as it is sometimes thought, exclusively to be applied in fashioning policy designed to deal with a recession or a depression, or more generally with deflationary tendencies in the economy. Keynes was by no means either 'left' in the ordinary political sense of the word or profligate as regards public finances. He was fully aware of the dangers of inflation and the benefit of prices being stable over a sufficiently long period of time. Nor can Keynes be regarded as being on one side or the other of the debate between private as against national enterprise or nationaliz-ation. If anything, given his whole liberal background, he was more likely to be in favour of enterprise by private individuals moved by what he called 'animal spirits' than by any opposite doctrine.

I have said that the heyday of macro-economics was probably to be found in the late fifties, sixties and early seventies of this century when on both sides of the Atlantic it gave rise to the principle of 'fine-tuning' on which many economists, particularly those who had been drawn into public administration, were inclined to place an enormous degree of confidence as regards the efficacy of the instruments at their disposal. This led to what I have described as hubris, after which inevitably nemesis would follow. The counter-revolution, as it were, that happened from the seventies onwards, as is so often the case, threw the baby out with the bathwater – that is to say, denigrated macro-economic policy as such rather than acknowledging its successes.

It is perhaps ironic that much of this counter-tendency, which was so prominent until quite recently in many countries, but more particularly in Britain, should have been dubbed the monetary counter-revolution and its advocates called monetarists. If ever there was an economist who had a strong view about the import-ance of money and monetary movements in fashioning the course of the economy as a whole, it was Keynes. His *Treatise on Money*

(1930) and *The General Theory of Employment, Interest and Money* (1936), apart from many earlier works, are eminent testimony to that fact.

Other Factors

Monetary policy has even before this innovation been a very powerful instrument of economic policy, going back a long time before even the First World War, when in general the banking system was largely governed by the Bank of England. The Central Bank was the sun of the planetary system round which the rest of the banking world was organized. The Bank of England exercised its powers by a variety of means, ranging all the way from the proverbial 'governor's eyebrows', the raising of which indicated to some party or other within the City's financial system that they were not behaving in the right sort of way, to changes in bank rate within the two specie points, which determined the inflow and outflow of gold and therefore the exchange rates, and also the abundance or the penury of money and credit within the system. Today, this whole apparatus has been much more systematized and is within the purview of the Monetary Policy Committee. The fact that the Monetary Policy Committee of the Bank of England is 'operationally' independent is itself a matter of some controversy and the actual action that the Committee takes to exercise its powers once a month is pretty hotly debated. Given the present almost lightning speed with which changes occur and are communicated through the media all round the financial community here and elsewhere, the expectation of changes itself is almost as important, and perhaps sometimes an even more important influence on financial movements than the changes themselves. I shall refer to this whole subject later, but for the moment I leave it that this is now one of the more important short-term measures at the disposal of the authorities for influencing the economic and financial climate.

I have already said something about the limits to the powers of the State in the economy, but it is worthwhile looking a little more closely at the balance between the activities of established organs of society, i.e. the State and other forms of collective authority, and what are nowadays called economic agents, that is to say individuals in the 'ordinary business of life'. In Western societies it is often thought that there have been changes in the extent to which authority prevails over the individual and vice versa. In fact in the last hundred years or more these fluctuations have been relatively slight. Except in wartime in Western societies the degree of authority exercised over what can be done by the individual has been relatively limited. In wartime of course the supply and application of labour, the use of raw materials and of plant and machinery, are very strictly controlled and subordinated to the purposes of the pursuit of war. In peacetime, however, with the exception of the command economies that to a substantial degree have now disappeared in Europe and to some extent even in the Far East and Latin America, the economic agents have had on the whole remarkably free room for manoeuvre.

It is sometimes thought that in recent decades – and again I speak primarily of this country and similar countries in the West – there has been a great tendency to abolish regulation, and deregulation has become the general fashion. I am not sure that these words are entirely appropriate to indicate what has happened. There is a substantial difference between the interference of authority to change the actual activities – and by that I mean primarily market activities – of individuals on the one hand, and on the other the authorities setting certain rules of the game within which the individual is free to do pretty well whatever he likes. If that distinction is made, then I think there has been a tendency to more rather than to less regulation, precisely because the direct intervention in markets by authority has diminished to a considerable extent and has very often totally disappeared. That, however, has at the same time created the need for rules of the game within which the individual can operate. Even these new rules are often not entirely novel. Many of them have existed before, although they have been laid down and enforced by self-regulation, often by organizations of individuals in professions and in various types of economic activity. Certainly in the financial field there has been a great deal of that, and this has now given way to a large extent to legislative provisions. Examples are the Bank of England Act and the new legislation that is due for setting up the Financial Services Authority. This will cover virtually the whole of the financial field and will take the place of what has earlier been self-regulation and later fragmentary regulation by the authority, sometimes not even backed by statute. The distinction I am making may not seem at first sight of great importance. However, it certainly is so because once one appreciates what is actually happening, it becomes clear that it is not so much a question of non-regulation versus regulation or deregulation, but rather a question of setting new goalposts to ensure a level playing field under proper rules of the game. The difference between them is that they also remove the quasi-ideological controversies that have often raged in the past between *dirigisme* and the free economy. Once the distinction I have made is realized, it will be seen that what has in fact happened is that the grounds for arguing about a *dirigiste* and a non-*dirigiste* economy are dwindling and, if present trends continue, may disappear altogether. This will certainly contribute to a more 'hygienic' form of intellectual debate in these matters.

The distinction I have made between active intervention in markets and regulation of markets so that individuals can look after their economic interests as best they can is an important one in considering how far we may expect spontaneous advantageous developments in the economy as technological change and other factors call for these, and how far actual intervention will still be needed. We can assume in the light of prevailing socio-political and cultural attitudes that there will be a general disinclination for active intervention in markets to take place. This is not to say that there will not be instances, certainly, of influence by governments to direct economic development in one way or another, for example where national interests are believed to be at stake, such as in the development of aircraft production and other industrial developments, particularly where they may have defence or foreign policy implications. There may even have to be from time to time a direct government investment. Generally, however, the kind of broad political attitude that existed in the Labour governments of the sixties and seventies – for example the tendencies to 'spot winners' and to support the industries thought to be in that category in some way either by government orders or by subsidies of one kind or another – will tend to be very rare indeed. The general framework, therefore, within which changes in the economy consequent upon other changes from outside or of a technological character within the economy itself have to be adapted, will tend to be judged by regulation of markets rather than by any more direct means. And the means will, broadly speaking, fall into the three categories which I have already mentioned, namely legislation where this is inevitable, and otherwise by fiscal and monetary policies of a more general character to affect the macro-economic climate.

The essence of the problem will be how far the economy will on its own show an adequate degree of adaptability (and an adaptability without very large time lags) to enable changes to be absorbed. This is a very difficult area to forecast, certainly over the next twenty years. For example, how far technological unemployment will continue to be an important factor cannot be assessed in an adequate time frame. It may well not be of very great importance over twenty years, although over a longer period it certainly will be; but in so far as it does emerge as an important problem over the current and the next parliament, it is very difficult to see how a government can avoid being drawn into the process of correcting the consequences by any means at its disposal, i.e. primarily fiscal and monetary policy. How far these means are effective is of course another matter, and despite any disinclination of an ideological character, which this government now shares with all the other major political tendencies in our country, remains to be seen. One can say that this will depend essentially on the decisions made by those most influential in determining the allocation of resources within the economy. It is not easy to say exactly where these powers lie. Clearly to a large extent they are within the decision-making powers and processes of large corporations that already control a substantial proportion of the gross domestic product of the country, some of them entirely British, some of them international. It does not make any substantial difference whether they are in fact multinational or indeed entirely foreign-controlled, or whether they are to a major degree or solely British-controlled. The important thing is to know in which direction their decisions are made to expand, or leave unchanged, or diminish any degree of industrial or commercial activity for which they are responsible, and how far new investment, the scrapping of old, the switching from one type of activity to another, are actually determined by them.

One can assume that in general they will be fairly responsive to the indications furnished by technological change that are likely to indicate the more against the less profitable lines of activity. Some time lag, some failure to assess properly the advantages and disadvantages of different types of enterprise, will arise and the adaptability will therefore not be perfect. On the other hand, one must assume the right kind of motivation and this is indeed the major factor that will determine the 'spontaneous' adaptability of the economy to change. Avoidance of loss and securing of profit is clearly the most potent motive available to economic enterprises of whatever character, whether they are large corporations or relatively small entities run primarily by one person or a small group of individuals – in other words, whatever their organization may be. I do not believe that actual experience – say, by looking at the history of the last two or three decades – gives one an unambiguous guide to how these motives and the decisions that spring from them will actually work out. There are many examples of major errors made by individual enterprises as well as of major successes. The reward for success or the punishment for errors is provided primarily by the market itself, i.e. by profit or loss; and where these are shown up in the results of corporate enterprises, they may take quite a while before they hit the shareholders sufficiently hard to cause changes in shareholders' reaction and, therefore, in share prices (up or down) with consequent redirection of the orientation of the enterprise itself. The process is there and corresponds much to what classic orthodox economics would lead one to expect. On the other hand, it is not a very effective and very smooth mechanism that can be expected to produce changes quickly and in proportion to the causes that call forth change. The prolonged bull market that we have experienced in recent years, and its correction when it comes, are certainly not an example of a very smooth and a very quick working mechanism of adaptation. The consequences of reorienting material and human resources away from erroneous decisions in the past and into future developments that promise better results is by no means guaranteed to take place with sufficient speed and without causing considerable losses of a material kind as well as great human distress through unemployment.

However, it would be wrong to expect the blemishes of the automatic economic adaptation system to be such as to lead to a major reversal of current tendencies and to a general acceptance of more direct intervention in markets. While the strict arguments that prevailed after the war between 'planners' and 'free marketeers' may have lost much of their intensity, there is still a great gap between absolute reliance on one as against absolute hankering for the other. On the whole, the likelihood is that for the next twenty years or more the justified disquiet over the efficacy of the spontaneous forces of the market will not grow to such an extent as to bring about a reversal of the present climate of opinion in these matters.

We must, therefore, expect that, good or bad, a high degree of reliance on spontaneous operation of market forces and the correction of errors will continue, and will probably be the most prevalent of the forces at work. Direct intervention for correcting past errors with the great risk of creating new ones will remain on the whole the exception rather than the rule unless a downward tendency of the economy creates such a rapid decline, and with it such a rapid development of discontent, that a general change of opinion with its political counterpart could reasonably be expected to take place. On the whole I think the chances remain over the next twenty years that this will not be the case.

At this point it must be emphasized that this problem of the extent to which market forces will themselves dominate and will continuously tend to establish their own equilibrium, even if this is not lasting and requires further correction, cannot be answered in general terms. Therefore, it will depend not only on developments within our own economy, but to an increasing extent on what happens in the world economy, and especially in the larger ones that have substantial influence on the general course of industrial and financial changes. This is not as easy to determine as one might think. It is true that there are certain outstanding world economies, notably that of the United States of America and – until recently – Japan too, that have a more than proportionate influence on the economies of other countries, including our own. But there is a continuous up and down in these matters and the changes over the last twenty years, for example as between the influence of Continental European economies and our own as compared with that of the United States, of Latin America and of the Commonwealth countries, has demonstrated that one cannot rely on a stable pattern in these matters. The future of the Continental European economies is now bound up with the start of the euro. Our non-membership of the EMU will therefore change what would otherwise have been a more 'normal' influence of the major Continental economies – German and French particularly – upon our own.

For the moment at any rate it can be observed that the difference between external economic influences and internal ones has grown much less in recent years, partly because of the internationalization of increasing segments of the world economy into entities incorporated on a multinational rather than a national basis. What used to be internal has become very much international and is, therefore, subject to decisions more strongly influenced by the views taken by those in charge of these international or multinational entities than was the case before. This is perhaps most strongly marked in the financial field, where the

movement of funds and the decisions in regard to these movements, both capital and short-term money, has become virtually
totally international rather than national. Of course national
decisions in regard to interest rates or fiscal policies and the
expectations which they create for the movement of foreign
exchanges, as well as for the movement of corporate profits within
different national markets, at present still exercise a major influence; but these are carefully weighed against each other, and those
who are taking the decisions now enjoy considerable freedom to
move from one set of decisions to another with ease and speed.

I do not wish to say that the decisions over the next twenty
years taken by our government will have no influence, or only a
very small one compared with what they had before. However, it
is still necessary to emphasize that their extent and weight will
be supplemented, or perhaps compensated for, by movements in
the world economy, particularly in that of the United States and
South-East Asia. To a minor degree, but at least psychologically,
what happens – as recent events have shown – in Russia and the
other emerging markets in Europe will also play a part.

This also means that leaving aside the 'spontaneous' forces in
the economy and looking more particularly on the room for
manoeuvre of government intervention or government policy generally, our government will, whatever its future desires may be,
have to take considerable account of what is happening elsewhere.
The extent to which it can itself exert influence through the
various international institutions, as well as by direct contact with
other countries, is subject to some limits; and they can be said to
have become more limited than they were certainly fifty years
ago. It is for example noteworthy – although it does not have a
direct impact on the question I have raised – that it is increasingly
difficult for British nationals to occupy major positions in international institutions. The World Bank, the International Monetary
Fund, the European Bank for Reconstruction and Development,
the World Trade Organization and so on (with the notable exception of the European Investment Bank at this stage) have not got
British nationals at their head or close to it. Although all these

organizations are supposed to be 'de-nationalized' in the sense that their leaders must subject allegiance to their own nationality to the institution they serve, nevertheless the influence, however indirect and difficult to assess, of their own previous national origin and the state of their own country does have some influence on the general conduct of their affairs.

PART THREE

Where Are We Going?

Phase One

The first Labour Conference since the party came to power was held fairly soon after the election and was therefore not much more than a celebration of victory. The second conference, held in September 1998, after the party had been in power for a year and a half, was a much more substantial affair.

The Prime Minister, as leader of the party, made a long and very elaborate speech covering practically every possible issue, constitutional, political, economic and administrative. It was extremely well received and there is very little doubt that this was not only the usual acclaim of the leader by the faithful – obligatory on these occasions – but seemed to be inspired by genuine and substantial shared belief and support for the sentiments expressed.

Subsequent commentators were also almost unanimously favourably impressed by the speech and there were only a few criticisms here and there. These almost exclusively turned on the question of what was the concrete content of the speech. It is true that it was largely a statement of intentions, beliefs and principles, and that precise suggestions for action by the government were few and far between. The speech also was criticized for containing, as is almost inevitable on these occasions, a great many slogans, some of which are unlikely to survive long after the party conference itself.

There is truth in much of this criticism. On the other hand, I think it would be not only churlish but naïve to criticize this kind of speech on the grounds that it is full of wonderful phrases but that there is very little concrete indication of the way in which the objectives that can be applauded are going to be achieved. I think it is naïve because a party conference is not a seminar in political science or even in political philosophy. Furthermore, it should be noted that the Prime Minister (and this has happened on earlier occasions at party conferences) left it very largely to his ministerial colleagues, who were well represented at the conference, to speak more specifically and in more detail about the programmes for which their own departments were going to be responsible.

It remains nevertheless true at that moment when the popularity of the government and of the Prime Minister was as high as it was to start with, and perhaps even higher, that the precise details of the party's action over the rest of this parliament and the one after had still to be largely sketched out.

Inevitably the attention of those who make a point of analysing their intellectual basis and the activities of the present government – leaving aside professional politicians and particularly professional political opponents – centre on the activities, public pronouncements and initiatives of the Prime Minister. These, at this time of writing have been of a rather mixed character. Sometimes they tend to carry with them a strong suggestion of PR purpose, image-making, etc. Let me say at once that much of this, even if justified, is not really a serious accusation against a professional politician. It is part and parcel of professional conduct, which none of them can really jettison completely without risk of ceasing to be politically effective. Indeed, although it may be argued that that aspect of a politician's life and work has become more prominent in the last few decades – I certainly would think so myself – that does not necessarily lead to a negative judgement. Politicians of recent years from Macmillan through Wilson to Blair, have all had a considerable dose of this. There have been some in the post-war period – Attlee for example, Jim Callaghan and to some degree even Major, though not Maggie Thatcher – who were rather less inclined to put the publicity and public relations aspect forward as strongly as the others have. Churchill of course was an entirely special case given his role in the War.

Almost as if the leadership of the party and the government had realized the lack of a coherent political pattern for what they stand for, a new concept has suddenly made its appearance, 'the third way'. It has not yet been clearly defined, but what is interesting is that it has evoked an echo across the Atlantic from President Clinton. It looks as though the Prime Minister and the President had agreed that the 'third way' represents something that they can both promote as a new political label.

It is apparently intended not only for their own followers in their own countries, but is to receive a broader launch in a gathering of 'leaders' from different countries, though this idea has at least for the moment disappeared. One of the problems is that while the label may convey something, indeed it is not entirely new: it echoes the 'middle way', a concept launched before the War and largely associated with Harold Macmillan and with the political ideas at the time of the 'left' and centre parties of the Scandinavian countries.

At any rate, it is not yet clear what the third way actually is. One suggestion is that it is something in-between complete private enterprise and complete nationalization. If so, it is very difficult to see what particular application, or indeed appeal, it might have in very many countries. Certainly in the Western European countries and in North America the ideological conflict that existed at one time between nationalization and private enterprise has largely ceased. The progress of privatization where nationaliz-ation had existed has been a dominant feature of economic development in the last two or three decades. It has taken place in various environments and in circumstances where the original nationalization that was to be replaced by private ownership was due to very different causes. In Mussolini's Italy it was quite different from what it was in post-First World War – and even more post-Second World War – Britain, or France after the War and then in the early days of the Mitterand administration. There may be arguments as to what to do with any enterprises that are still wholly or to a large extent in state ownership, but these are matters more of a technical financial character than of doctrine. Of course in countries like China the state enterprises are still predominant, but even there their number is shrinking, any delay often due to unfavourable market conditions making the placing of shares difficult.

The third way does not seem to me to have much new political appeal either in the United States or in France – though for different reasons. Even in our country, for reasons that I have already touched upon in regard to the general complexion of our main parties, the appeal of a third way, i.e. something between two other – more extreme – ways, is very hard to visualize. It may in fact be argued that in many countries, certainly in the most developed industrialized ones, the third way is already a fact. Neither extreme ideology has really still got a great deal of support and, therefore, political appeal. Obviously nuances of difference remain, leaning a little bit more towards one direction rather than another. Nor can one yet be sure that this bland situation will persist.

The government has emphasized that it is, and intends to continue to be, 'business-friendly'. Whether the implication that 'old' Labour was not – or was perhaps even 'business-hostile' – is debatable. However, that apart, the question is what exactly 'business-friendly' means. The government, like all previous governments in the last sixty years or so, including many previous Labour governments, has, and must have, close contacts with leading businessmen. Leaders of business are often of two kinds. There are those who are imaginative, innovative, with a relentless pursuit of fresh ideas, determined to do the best for their firm, which means for their customers, their employees and their shareholders; men who are not averse to receiving suitable rewards for their efforts and their successes, but are nevertheless primarily motivated by the success of the enterprise which they run. There are unfortunately also others, leaders, so-called, of business, who are essentially skilful navigators on the corporate seas. They are able boardroom politicians; they know how to establish a name in the City and in business circles generally by various devices; they know how to create at an early stage in their career, as it were, a benchmark for the emoluments that they believe to be due to them in terms of salary, bonuses, pension rights, options and other 'goodies'. For them very often, when one considers the history of the enterprises they have presided over, it would, alas, be true to say that failure is the best road to personal success.

This, however, is a relatively secondary aspect of the problem of relations between government and business on a personal basis. More important is the broad policy of the government for business purposes. And here – we have discussed this at quite some length already in various ways – it may be relevant to look at the effect of different government policies on individual businesses. This is particularly so where the original establishment of the business, or its development, has been largely due to government support, intervention or at least government promotion, and where subsequent failure does bring disaster for many innocent victims, employees who lose their jobs, management who stand to be convicted of failure and shareholders who lose money.

But in a wider sense, for government to create a climate in which business in the best and broadest sense of the word – that is to say, enterprise designed to create growth, employment and a higher standard of living – is very relevant indeed. Here it would be quite wrong to suppose that business-friendliness is an entirely new invention of this government. All governments in the past, even those of a more left-wing character than we are likely to encounter in the foreseeable future, have been primarily motivated, and have so professed themselves to be, by the desire to foster economic well-being through better economic performance and consequently growth.

Still, 'business-friendly' may be a convenient and possibly politically advantageous slogan, particularly when paraded at the start of a new government, especially one of a Labour Party that has not had the opportunity to govern the country for eighteen years. The difficulty is that for some aspects of government–business relations it is extremely difficult for a government to show friendliness that is not orientated towards one particular business or type of business and that, therefore, may well more often than not call forth an opposite reaction from other businesses. Unless the government is prepared to intervene directly, which is, as we have seen, broadly against its political stance, the general economic climate that it is trying to create must be of a universal character and cannot as a rule specifically favour this or that business enterprise. There is a major dilemma here, which will no doubt show up in various ways, particularly when it comes to intervening in certain proposals made within the business community itself, such as mergers and acquisitions of all kinds where ultimately the government's decision may be required. There have been suggestions that the government, or at least the Department of Trade and Industry, may abandon its powers of veto over take-overs. It is very difficult to see how this can be universal. There will always remain certain areas, for example in regard to defence, where a government decision whether to allow some particular reconstruction of a corporate character to go forward or not cannot be avoided.

What has become known as 'globalization' is another aspect of modern economic development that makes it increasingly difficult for the government to be always its own master in deciding not only on specifics, but even often on broad lines of policy (again for example in regard to mergers and acquisitions), as well as anything that involves international capital markets. It is a matter of considerable concern in many areas whether some degree of broader international concerted and co-operative intervention may be needed, particularly in the light of the volatility of capital markets that has been so evident since the Asian crises and the troubles that the emerging markets, particularly Russia and Latin America, have recently gone through.

There is perhaps a parallel here in the deregulation of industry and its privatization (very often where it had been in state owner-ship and/or management) and the need to preserve some degree of supervision over these newly privatized enterprises, particularly where they concern public utilities. The parallel here is with the great deregulation and liberalization of international developments in regard to mergers and acquisitions and the consequent capital movements, with investors being in a position now to move their investments quite freely most of the time across national boundaries. What is perhaps even more important is that alongside 'genuine' investors, those who dispose of very large funds can move them across frontiers according to their beliefs in the future development of currencies, interest rates and stock markets with the greatest of ease and at lightning speed.

It may be appropriate here to add some reflection on the most recent developments in three economies, one of which has already had a considerable influence on the rest of the world, including our country, and the other two potentially so. This is particularly appropriate since the world economies in general are more closely connected compared with what was the case a few years ago. They are faced with relatively new problems, which are different and virtually the exact opposite of those with which they have had to grapple before, namely those of inflation. This is in any event a question of what is the right economic policy for our own country, but since 1996 at least it has affected much of the world, both the so-called emerging markets, the second largest world economy of Japan and much of the developed world, including Western Europe. Many countries have experienced a downturn and the possibility of recession/depression is now a world-wide concern.

It is therefore pertinent to look, for example, at Japan, the troubles of which certainly exceed in terms of world relevance those of the rest of Asia and particularly South-East Asia. They have a direct impact on much of the economy of the developed world, including our own. Here the paradox is that Japan is faced with the possible necessity of pursuing what would normally be regarded as two entirely opposite policies. On the one hand there is the question of what to do about the financial system, which is the most seriously troubled at the moment and threatened with spreading bankruptcies. This has already started both in brokerage houses and in banks as distinct from the industrial economy, which, although in the doldrums, is showing signs of preserving some of its traditional strength and resilience. Here, as far as finance is concerned, opinions differ considerably. There is the argument that if you do not bail out some of these financial institutions, perhaps all of them, you will aggravate the 'domino effect' and create such chaos and deflationary pressure that it will be virtually impossible to wait for the recovery. On the other hand there is the argument that the bailing-out of a large part of the financial system will absorb large amounts of funds that would be available to the government for other purposes and will merely prolong the agony. It is impossible to judge this question on an overall basis and only those closely in touch with the system can decide which institutions it would be essential to preserve and support and which should be allowed to go to the wall.

Whatever is decided on this score, what is quite clear is that on the other side the correct prescription for Japan is something that can only be described as Keynesian demand stimulus. Both consumer demand and investment must be stimulated and that can normally only be done by fiscal and monetary policy. On the score of monetary policy much has already been done and short-term interest rates are practically 'invisible'. Whether it will be effective or not is as yet not clear; nor have the large funds appropriated for general economic stimulus as yet produced significant results. Thus, on the fiscal front too, as well as on the more direct financial support that would quickly flow into investment, consumer demand and employment, there is no decisive sign yet that the government's policy has succeeded.

It is a very difficult situation indeed for which there is no real precedent and the Western governments, particularly the United States, who keep urging Japan to do this or that are not always sufficiently conscious of the difficulties, particularly in a country with the social and political structure of Japan, to do the right thing at this stage.

There is no doubt in my mind that, apart from the economic and financial problems of Japan, many of their difficulties at the moment stem from the fact that its social and political structure, which has obviously already undergone great changes this century, is nevertheless basically not attuned to the requirements of a modern economy. This is particularly so in regard to the party system, the programmes of the parties, and the extent to which the electorate is aware of these programmes and divided in its allegiance. A further factor is the relationship of the bureaucracy to the political classes. All this is still very much as it has been for the last fifty years or more and that has, I think, created quite a discrepancy between the modernity of industry and finance and the traditional nature of society as a whole. It is by no means the case that in matters of, as it were, cultural, religious and general social conduct, there needs to be any great change in Japan, and it does not at all follow that in their domestic habits and customs they need to turn themselves overnight into, as it were, a mid-Western American type of society. It is true that to some extent this has been the case in many matters: diet, for example, where there have been very considerable approximations to Western habits and standards. Nevertheless, one still has the feeling that in many fundamental respects the political and administrative system remains imbued with principles and practices that may be admirable in themselves, but are not entirely consistent with the requirements of a modern industrial and financial society. It is often said that one of the problems that Japan faces is that decision-making in all areas of society – government, administration and business at all levels – is completely dominated by the principle of consensus, and this is something different from and more far-reaching than what one might call democratic decision-making by voting or otherwise ascertaining a majority opinion. It is something that goes much deeper and is therefore more likely to impede quick decision and quick changes of direction of policy. It is like turning round a battleship rather than a cruiser and, therefore, whatever may be required by the adoption of modern financial, industrial and commercial practices may not always as quickly as is necessary be reflected in the surrounding social, administrative and political landscape. It is very difficult to ascertain whether this is true, and in any event it is hardly directly relevant to my main theme, but it is because of the size of the Japanese economy and its influence on the rest of the world, including our country, that it is necessary to refer to it. Moreover, the way in which – so far at least – traditional economic policies have worked shows that these cannot in all circumstances have the effects desired. Nevertheless, I think it necessary to add here that I do not share the pessimistic views that are sometimes derived from this kind of analysis of Japan's economic future. Decisions may take more time, but the inherent strength of the Japanese economy will, I believe, produce the necessary upturn.

The other area by which at present the world economy appears to be influenced, and perhaps threatened, is Russia, potentially the biggest economy of the so-called emerging markets, at any rate outside China and Latin America. Russia since the fall of the Soviet regime has been moving at a quite rapid pace towards adopting Western economic and financial institutions and methods, including liberalization, privatization, deregulation and rapid dismantling of what was known as the command economy. This has, not surprisingly, been accompanied by a good deal of economic growth as well as not only 'cronyism', as it is sometimes called, but also corruption and downright crime, including Mafia-type practices and institutions. This is to some degree, I believe, very difficult, if not impossible, to avoid altogether. It may probably be what was taking place two or three hundred years ago in our own Western societies when capitalism first developed and flourished.

The situation has, however, been aggravated in Russia by the very rapid, indeed much more rapid, dismantling of the political and administrative framework that surrounded and sustained the old command economy. While to Western ideas that was a highly desirable development and while many of the features of the old Soviet regime, particularly in the earlier days of Stalin and Brezhnev were repugnant and repulsive to Western thought, nevertheless one has to recognize that it did provide some kind of framework for the economy. The transformation of that economy towards a capitalist, largely free-market economy, while at the same time the social and the political framework completely disappeared, as it did in Russia, and was not replaced quickly enough by a Western system, presents very considerable problems. It could be argued that one of the less desirable features of the old system, the so-called privileged position of the 'nomenclatura', was simply taken over by a new group not based on the party, which enjoyed privileges of a capitalist nature and freedoms of behaviour that were certainly not the Western pattern. This included of course the absence, or at least the very, very slow development, of a legal system suitable in all respects to the new economic trends.

It does go well beyond the theme of this particular study, but it is worth referring to the difference between the development in this respect of Russia and of China. In China, perhaps to the regret of many people in the West, the administrative and political framework, including the legal system and the relative absence – perhaps originally the almost complete absence – of individual freedom, was of course highly distasteful. To some extent this has been remedied and continues to be improved, but the general framework still remains and it is perhaps significant that as it remains it provides a rather more stable framework for the development of a freer, deregulated, liberalized, increasingly market-oriented economy. This of course still has a very long way to go in China, but it has made remarkable progress and has not led – at least not to anything like the same extent as it has in Russia – to the less desirable features of that development that I have mentioned above.

This short excursion into the problems of the second largest economy of the world, Japan, with some reflections on Russia and China, will certainly be relevant to our own development because of their influence directly on our own economy through trade and finance as well as because Japanese recovery can make a major difference to the course of economic development in Asia, particularly South-East Asia. Russia, and even more China, have a more distant relation with our own economic fate. They do, however – say, in the course of the next parliament – begin to be more relevant if only through the gathering pace of economic globalization, a process that, unless some political or economic catastrophe rekindles a move towards economic nationalism, will be a major force. This will be particularly important in fashioning the broader economic choices our country will need to make in the second decade of the period under review.

Meanwhile, our present government has yet to complete its programme for the first parliament and then to face the problems of another quinquennium, if it is re-elected. At this, almost the half-way stage of its first period in power, some of the 'side effects' of a huge majority begin to appear, leaving aside altogether the inevitable 'local difficulties' besetting even important ones of its members.

First in narrow circles of those who follow politics, then in wider ones, there is an inevitable demand to show 'what have you done'. As I have already said, the government has been far from idle. I have indicated many areas in which action has been taken and the number of consultative documents, White Papers, including policy statements and actual legislative proposals, have been many. Nevertheless, the populace as a whole, particularly under the influence of the press, will still ask, 'What about the London Underground?' or 'What about the "Freedom of Information Act"?' Impending reform of the House of Lords, however important in the long term – and a firm manifesto commitment – is not a very effective substitute. Inevitably the government's rhetoric is scrutinized and contrasted with its actions.

This has been aggravated by something I have already mentioned, namely the appearance of a public relations purpose as distinct from, and perhaps superior to, the substantive purpose of what is proposed. All governments run risks in this regard. For the present one it carries with it the danger of creating scepticism or even indifference. One example in the government's relatively early days was the proposal to create a new super-class of 'consultant nurses'. This in itself is a proposal for which merit can be rightly claimed. On the other hand, as it was made at a time when on all sides, and not only by the parties affected, the pay and conditions of nurses were regarded as lamentably too low – and indeed had resulted in great recruitment difficulties and a substantial lack of adequate numbers of nurses – the proposal inevitably carried with it a suggestion that it was meant as a diversion from the real need – however unjustified that may have been.

On the other hand, there can be very little doubt about the sincerity of the Prime Minister's concern with urban housing and particularly with the growth of foci of crime, as well as deprivation and general decline in certain housing estates. A proposal to devote £800 million to wipe out these foci to improve many of the housing estates, and where improvement is not possible to do away with them altogether, can only be welcomed as one of the major achievements when it is actually implemented and is one that would certainly not be criticized by even the most 'old' of 'old Labour' partisans.

The other concerns of government in general that go outside the economic sphere are hardly to be classified as distinguishable between old Labour or socialist ideas and New Labour with its relatively neutral stance in questions of this kind. These concern for example such matters as the decriminalization of certain types of drugs such as cannabis or the attitude to student grants, some of these matters being within the purview of the Home Office, which has certainly shown itself under its present minister to be less ready to move than might have appeared likely when Labour was in opposition. On the other hand, these are not really matters that much concern those who still preserve some of the concepts of what divides socialist from non-socialist ideas. They are of a much more general character, and partisans and antagonists are to be found distributed more or less at random between the different political attachments.

More directly significant in this connection is the relationship between the government and the trade unions, which as I have already described earlier, have lost a good deal of their power together with their membership. In the last nearly twenty years the membership has dropped from about 13 million to just under 7 million and rather significantly the vast majority of the members are to be found in public sector employments rather than in the private sector. Yet it is precisely in the public sector that successive governments, including the present one, have been particularly rigorous in restraining wages or other cost-raising factors while in the private sector – often to the distress of the government and the monetary authorities – there has been a fairly steady improvement. It has often gone beyond compensating for the actual rate of inflation, let alone sticking to the inflation target set by the government.

However, this is not to say that the government is antagonistic to the trade unions. While the relationship may not be as intimate or as overtly close as it has been from time to time – not only in the distant past but also under some Labour governments this century, particularly the Wilson government – and while it may be more at 'arm's length', it nevertheless continues to be significant. A trace of the old umbilical cord that tied the Labour Party to the trade unions is still visible from time to time and the Labour Party still relies a good deal on them for moral and material support. Moreover, the government has actually shown by deed a desire to take into account the concerns of trade unions, for example in the recognition of trade union bargaining with employers and also in the passing of the minimum wage legislation. I have referred to both these already at an earlier stage in connection with economic policy.

The government is also committed to accept the provisions of the Social Chapter of the European Union, although not necessarily *in toto*. More particularly the provision for consultation with the workforce in enterprises that employ more than a certain number of workers (at present twenty) is one that the government has more or less indicated it will not accept. Whether this is wise or necessary is difficult to determine. The experience on the Continent where not only consultation as provided for by the European Directive exists but where indeed works councils and worker representation on boards are quite common, e.g. in France and Germany, there is no evidence that this has hampered management in its proper tasks. Indeed, it is argued that now and again, from the trade unions' or the workers' point of view at any rate, they have been so ineffective as to be virtually insignificant. Sometimes, however, they seem to have contributed to improving relations; and it could be thought that, particularly in times of pressure when economic conditions require considerable restructuring of working conditions and also create redundancies, they can play a useful part. A machinery for consultation with the workforce that has been practised for some time and is accepted by both sides could be useful in times when consensus is a necessary condition for the adoption of economically difficult measures.

To the end of this parliament, i.e. to the year 2002, we can assume that the course that this government will follow is set, though always subject to unforeseen shocks, sometimes originating quite outside major policy areas. However, there will be some quite major developments, which I have already indicated. First of all, the new spending programme of £40 billion for education and health will begin to come into effect. This will obviously come gradually, but if the government is serious about it, then over three years – that is to say, until the next election in 2002 – a great deal of it, perhaps all of it, will have been implemented. It will have an important effect, the nature of which it is too difficult to outline here and now, on the way in which education as well as health, those two great public services, are actually carried on in our country. Beyond that, they will have a macro-economic effect because of whatever other manipulation there may be in the next two or three budgets: it is impossible to accommodate that kind of spending programme without affecting the whole of the tax and spending stance of the government. What is certain is that this will give rise to much political debate both inside the government and the ruling party and in the political arena generally, and may furnish important ammunition to the opposition in its effort to revive itself. It will concern what effect on taxing and spending it will actually bring about and what concomitant changes in personal and corporate tax, direct and indirect, as well as in other spending programmes, including foreign affairs and defence, will follow from it. So this is an area that, being highly debatable, will form one important part of political controversy.

If I am right about this, then to some extent at least, the present paucity of aspects of broad economic policy on which the two main political parties may disagree and perhaps fight the next election will give way to much more lively and more substantive debate.

On the other hand, looking ahead to 2002, it is very difficult to discern now exactly what might become the principal arena in which the two main parties will seek the favour of the electorate. Up to now, the stance of the government has been such that it has really been quite difficult for the main opposition party, the Conservatives, to pick very many holes in it. Of course, there are always certain specific aspects of this or that action, of this legislation or that, of this change in regulation or that, for instance in regard to welfare provisions and benefits, on which a political case against the government may be made. But, broadly speaking, it looks as though the present arena, if it were to continue virtually unchanged until 2002, may leave really only two great issues on which there may be a major fight between the two parties. One is constitutional reform, particularly in regard to Scotland and Wales and the creation of new assemblies – to a minor degree also the new government that is contemplated for London and possibly for other major cities. I do not think in this connection that House of Lords reform will form a major issue. In addition there will be the great question of Europe. This is *par excellence* the issue on which at any rate the Conservative Party has taken a well-defined and quite clear-cut stance, as of now, which it is committed to maintain until the year 2007, that is to say for this parliament and the next. The government has not taken a clear-cut opposite position, but all the indications are that it certainly does not share the opposition to the Single Currency – and what may follow from it – that the Tory Party has embraced. Indeed a number of members of the government are credited with a more forthcoming attitude to Europe as I have already indicated earlier. It may well be that by the time we reach 2002 Europe, rather than the constitutional issues, will form the major battleground. The outcome of this battle is uncertain at this moment. However,

I will make what I consider a reasonably safe guess. It is highly unlikely that the British electorate will be prepared by 2002 to accept that for another five years we must stay outside. On the other hand, to produce the acceptance in the electorate will clearly be a very tough job, largely, I think, because the government has for much too long neglected preparing the ground. The time is getting shorter and the difficulties of swinging public opinion, not all of it by a long way, but enough of it to create a positive result in the referendum, are becoming greater. The media are predominantly still lined up against joining as they have been all along. One or two of them that have been favourable, or at least benevolently neutral to favourable, have as a result of the introduction of the euro come out a bit more strongly in favour. But those that have been opposed, particularly the two run by the two great media moguls and their satellite newspapers, remain hostile and continue to agitate against. The Tory Party itself shows no sign of changing, judging by the attitude of its leader and the two or three principal spokesmen who joined Mr Hague precisely on the occasion of the introduction of the euro to reaffirm their total opposition to our joining, at any rate for the next eight years.

I believe that this will be one of the major preoccupation of the government quite outside the legislative machine, but it will certainly greatly affect the line-up for the next election.

Apart from that there are certain things that are obviously going to occupy parliament and form a major part of the legislative programme. One is House of Lords reform. It is not quite clear yet when and where it will first be introduced, but there are a great many discussions going on between groups of peers and the government, either formally or informally, to decide, for example, on the methods of choosing the ninety-one or so hereditary peers who (in an earlier proposal), for the time being until total House of Lords reform has come about, will remain in the House and have the right to vote. Similarly already there are discussions going on about the composition and terms of reference of the Royal Commission that will recommend the ultimate shape of the House. The chairman has already been appointed and rumours are current about preferences the Prime Minister is supposed to have as to the ultimate shape of the Upper Chamber – that is to say, as regards the division between elected and nominated peers. But all this is total speculation at the moment. What I think is certain is that before the next election there may well be a small component of hereditary peers in the House of Lords with only a limited life, and probably only appointed peers, even if the ultimate reform contains provision for elected peers.

Of other legislative programmes one that is of considerable importance to the economy will be the Financial Services Bill. This is not yet introduced as I am writing this (although a preliminary draft has been in existence for some months), but will be of very great importance not only because it will more clearly define the powers of the Financial Services Authority, but also because it is bound to lay down in greater detail, and over a more extensive area, the rules of conduct for the financial services industry, given the great importance that industry has in our economy, led by the City of London, some of which I have already mentioned. It will also be important because the kind of parameters it consists of and the kind of limits it lays down for different types of conduct in different areas of financial services will demarcate the powers and functions and role of the City of London vis-à-vis the other markets that will develop inside Euroland. Since it is at the moment unfortunately unlikely that we shall join Euroland before the next election, it does mean that until 2002–2003 whatever emerges from the financial services industry will have a very important bearing on the competitive position of the City of London compared with Frankfurt and possibly the other less important financial centres of Euroland.

For the rest, what might happen before 2002 that lies within the purview of our government and our own actions on the assumption that we shall still be members of the European Union, but not members of Euroland, the following might be said. In a report of the House of Lords Select Committee on European Affairs two or three years ago, which discussed the policies of the 'outsiders' and the 'insiders' of the Single Currency zone, it was pointed out that even if we are outside the euro-zone, we shall, for reasons that are carefully set out in the report, to a very large extent have to follow in regard to macro-economic management very similar policies to those that obtain inside Euroland. The main argument is that it would be quite impossible for us for competitive reasons to follow markedly distinct policies as regards the fiscal and monetary policy, including the effect that the latter in particular would have on the exchange rate of sterling to the euro. If this argument is correct, as I think it is, then the justification for staying 'outside' for reasons of 'national independence' in these matters becomes even more untenable.

To return to the broader aspects of economic policy, it must be said that, as far as the last two years are concerned, this is a puzzling subject. The purpose of strategy, if strategy there is, is not easily discernible, nor is it very clear what function the various instruments that have been used, notably fiscal and monetary policy, are meant to fulfil in achieving whatever that strategy is. To this extent the policy of the present government does not differ very materially from that of its predecessor, which was also considerably unclear and to a large extent appeared to have been concocted on a very ad hoc basis. There are certain elements of the present policy – such as the fiscal stance adopted by the Chancellor or the conferment of independence for the fixing of short-term interest rates on the Monetary Policy Committee of the Bank of England and the policy that this body has subsequently followed – that are fairly evident. What is not at all clear is what they were meant to achieve and what they have in fact achieved. There has been a certain appearance of self-satisfaction at our position, for example in relation to the state of our economy compared with that of most of our partners in the European Union. The latter has been described – and not only by opponents of our joining the euro, to whom this is a powerful argument – as being inferior to our own. There is very little real evidence of that. It may be that in the immediate past our position was somewhat better than that of our Continental neighbours, but much of that advantage seems to have disappeared. One concept that has suddenly become very fashionable is that of the economic cycle. This is an old economic concept that was not used very much in economic theory and in economic debate for many years, but has recently been revived and is used to describe not only changes in our own situation – although this is not always very clearly identified in terms of the economic cycle – but more in comparison with the situation vis-à-vis some particular economic cycle – again not clearly identified – on the Continent. It is certainly used quite a lot by opponents of our joining the euro, including even some who are not absolutely against it but have simply adopted a wait-and-see attitude. And this applies to some of our authorities, political as well as otherwise. We are told that our position in the economic cycle is different from that of the Continent and that that makes it very difficult to join the euro. If we look ahead to the immediate future from the beginning of 1999, which is when I am writing this, then we do find that for example we now have short-term interest rates nearly double those (3%) that the European Central Bank has adopted for Euroland. They are $5\frac{1}{2}$ % at the moment, and even though they may go down in the near future, they will still remain considerably higher than on the Continent for quite some time. Our unemployment has risen somewhat in recent months, though it has now also fallen, but the short-term fluctuations here and on the Continent do not really provide an unambiguous picture. The outlook for the growth of gross domestic product is certainly inferior here to what it is on the Continent. Our own estimates now run at under 1 per cent for 1999, which is very much less than was forecast only a short time ago. Our manufacturing industry is in a bad state, partly as a result of the difficulties experienced by the export industries. As for these, they had of course suffered a very severe blow from the high pound – in part brought about by the restrictive monetary policy of high short-term interest rates. Although the rate of exchange to the mark had got considerably lower than it was at one time (when it reached three marks), i.e. about 2.72 (at the time of the creation of the euro), it is still considerably higher than most experts would regard as appropriate in terms of the normal functioning of our export industries without the benefit of any competitive devaluation of the pound.

So altogether it seems that we have not managed our affairs all that well in terms of growth, in terms of employment, in terms of manufacturing industry and in terms of interest rates. That last element might be remedied somewhat by the expected further reduction in short-term interest rates.

We are thus entering the second phase of this government's first parliament in an economic condition that is far from brilliant. This is particularly worrying at a time when it is quite obvious that many of the ideas that the government has, many of its projects and perhaps those that it has left on one side but may be forced to look at again, such as taxation, with a somewhat more redistributive character, and also a major reform of the welfare system, perhaps including the tax and benefits system combined, are going to be much more difficult to bring about in a situation in which growth and employment are at best stagnating, if not declining. This presents a very serious problem for the government, although there is no great evidence yet that the opposition is making, or indeed can make, much capital out of the situation. Indeed for some time it looked as though in strictly economic terms they would have to do little more than nibble at the edges of economic policy and content themselves primarily with attacking the government on the question of Europe. However, if the government is not very careful, it may well land itself in a situation, come the 2002 election, in which its economic policy itself has produced a situation in which, justly or unjustly, it may be more vulnerable to the attacks of the opposition.

In looking at the course of action of the Monetary Policy Committee as shown in their reports to date, which are, if not totally revealing, nevertheless a pretty full source of information, one cannot escape the conclusion that on the whole the Committee, in terms of its voting, at any rate, has been oversensitive to the danger of inflation and certainly not sufficiently alert to the turn-around in the situation that has made deflation a more imminent danger. This could be made to a considerable degree responsible for the general character of our economic policy with the consequences that I have described above. Of course it is by no means an indictment of the Monetary Policy Committee as such. I think one may say about the Monetary Policy Committee what used traditionally to be seen in the Western saloon, 'Don't shoot the pianist, he is only doing his best.' The real problem arises from the fact that the Monetary Policy Committee has been given far too lonely a position in the general structure of economic policy and has been endowed with just one instrument of policy for that purpose, namely the variation of short-term interest rates. Moreover, 'inflation targeting', regarded as a sort of British mono-poly and as the only source of wisdom in these matters, should not have been, in my view, pursued in this doctrinal manner. The phrase 'inflation-targeting' is itself misleading. The remit of the MPC is to secure price stability. 'Inflation-targeting' contains an implied assumption of the main danger to stability. Moreover, price indices, apart from difficulties of measurement, are not the only important factor. Indeed, the latest reports of the Monetary Policy Committee show that it itself to a large extent moved from exclusive attention to the level of 'permissible' price changes as set by the Chancellor and has taken into account many other factors before coming to its conclusions.

Phase Two

The difficulty of dealing with Phase Two is that one has first to get over the hurdle of the next election, that is presumably in 2002. I have already said that in my opinion almost certainly Labour will win that election and come to power and, therefore – other things being equal – be in office for another parliament, i.e. to the end of my first decade. One must assume also that while Labour will have an adequate majority to last – again other things being equal – the whole of that quinquennium, that majority will not be as large as it is now. There is no guarantee about this, but in the normal course of things it is highly unlikely that any government, however successful in its first term, could command quite so crushing a majority over its opponents the second time round. Unless the Conservative Party shows considerable ineptness – which of course is not excluded – in readjusting itself to the new situation, one can assume that they will recover some, but not a substantial part, of the lost ground.

Thus, for practical purposes the most reasonable assumption is a Labour government roughly of the same complexion as now under the leadership of Mr Blair and commanding a considerable, though not an overwhelming, majority in parliament. The qualifications that I have made arise first of all from the conduct both of the government and of the main opposition party between now and 2002, and secondly from the absence of any cataclysmic developments after 2002 that would make the possibility of Labour lasting the whole of that parliament unlikely. However, I will ignore these two possibilities for the purpose of the analysis that follows.

I also leave out of account the possibility of substantial changes in the Upper Chamber affecting the above assumptions. First of all, whatever the reform of the House of Lords, it is unlikely to be completed before 2002. Furthermore, any radical change in the powers of the new House vis-à-vis the Commons is also unlikely.

One can never forecast exactly what will be the main issues at a general election, but I have already indicated that this will turn mainly on our European policy, particularly since the present government is committed – if it reaches a favourable conclusion on the subject – to seek the approval of the people in a referendum for our joining the Single Currency, say, towards the end of 2002 or early in 2003.

I speculate in the next section on the likely attitude of the political parties to the European 'problem' in the longer term. Even if the referendum is carried, it is, on present indications, not excluded that the Tory Party will continue antagonistic – apart from the question of adopting the euro – since 'the people will have spoken'; but there could be much opposition on detail and on further developments.

Substantial electoral battles in 2002 over other matters are not to be excluded, depending to a considerable extent not only on the government's rating with the people at large, but also on how far the government has been able to satisfy the bulk of its own followers, including those who are not yet totally committed to supporting 'New' Labour.

Another difficulty – paradoxically – that makes 2002–2007 more difficult to deal with than the second half of my period under review is precisely that it is much closer at hand. Further away, the analyst is a 'chartered libertine'. Three years from the ensuing parliament is much more determined by forces already at work.

What then are likely to be the second Labour government's preoccupations? In part, the agenda is clear: unfinished business. It is inevitable that some, perhaps much, of the government's programme during its first term will not be finished before the dissolution. Even in its first two years, the output of bills, White Papers, consultative papers and other statements of policy reviews and intentions has been formidable. The next three years will produce more. Even if Lords Reform, Food Standards Agency and Freedom of Information, to mention only a few that are pending, have come on to the statute book, much legislation on many broad issues may not. In so far as the government has these at heart, it will wish to complete them – and so indicate in its 2002 electoral manifesto.

Much else in the economic and financial sphere, quite apart from legislation, such as the Financial Services Bill, may run into 2003 and thereafter. Probably the biggest issue that will also determine much of the manifesto (and the ensuing electoral battle) will concern benefits and the longer-term pattern of taxing and spending.

Some of the matters of a more economic character – for example, a review of the government's attitude to competition, which includes mergers, acquisitions and take-overs, and the general structure of monopoly and fair trading regulation that exists at the moment – will probably be reviewed. There are already signs that the DTI is considering the issue of how far government should intervene in these matters through one or other of these agencies. Whatever the outcome may be of our internal discussions on this before the end of the present parliament, it is quite clear that on this and many other similar matters we shall have to have regard to what is happening in Europe generally. Certainly in the next parliament and by the time we are members of Euroland, we will need to take account of whatever has been discussed and later decided within the European Union. It is quite certain that the European Union will concern itself with these problems, which are to some extent related to the creation of a 'level playing field' in order to sustain the Single Market.

The government's avowed intentions on some of these issues have been quite ambitious, but generally they have not tackled them head-on with overall solutions. This is understandable. On many of these problems, overall solutions are intellectually and politically hugely contentious. Moreover, if misjudged, they can have serious consequences, which are difficult to undo. It is unlikely that this will have changed greatly when we reach the second phase. Whether commitment to a broader programme for the second parliament will appear electorally advantageous is hard to say. Much depends on how far the as yet small indications of pressure from its left wing will have developed in the next three years. Apart from that, the government may need to demonstrate something more novel to give it a 'second wind' for its second term. My guess is that these factors will weigh quite heavily and that something as novel in appearance as 'New' Labour was in 1997 will be needed, without, however, giving the impression of a reversion to 'old' Labour: a very delicate operation!

I speculate in the next section among other things on the Prime Minister's recently pronounced belief that we shall before very long become a middle-class society. If this is really to influence, let alone determine, the government's general programme and action, then I think a start will have to be made during the second parliament. How far this somewhat nebulous concept can be translated into a programme of governmental action, including perhaps legislation, it is difficult to see. Education and health have a major influence on lifestyle and on the actual position enjoyed by large sections of the community. Steps have already started in the present parliament and will clearly have to be continued in the next. A related matter, which has a particular influence on this question of the middle-class society, as well as on much more direct aspects of the government's position, is the treatment of public employees. As I write this, the government has just announced certain important changes in the wage structure of teachers and nurses, two categories of public employment that are not only very important, but which, as a result of various mis-judged experiments of recent decades and of considerable neglect of the needs of these employees, have created quite a critical situation. Recruitment in particular has been falling. It is quite clear already that the steps taken by the government now are – as is inevitably the case – pleasing to some but also very much rejected by others. These are matters of extraordinary difficulty as far as governments are concerned and require a great deal of foresight in order to create structures of wages and conditions for public employees that will be appropriate for the longer term. This is not simple because demand is not easy to forecast and the relative position of these particular employees in relation to others in the public service, let alone in private employment, is changing and requires from time to time adjustment to keep the original purposes still valid.

These matters too, I think, will need to be tackled more systematically in the second parliament. They will be part, I believe, of a more general review of the whole policy of the government – not neglecting the private sector either – to rewards and emoluments in relation to the needs of society. However much one may believe – and this government does so to a considerable extent – in letting these matters be settled by market forces, it is quite clear that this is not always enough in practical terms. The trouble is that we do not start with a clean sheet and what has been done by governments twenty years earlier has its consequences, which cannot be ignored and dealt with simply on the basis of first principles. This is part of a problem with which I deal more in the next section, namely the whole question of redistribution of income and wealth in so far as the government might be prepared by that time to consider this more seriously. To emphasize this at this stage is not to ignore market forces entirely and to believe that everything can be settled by legislation or by government first. Indeed, even such obvious blemishes of our society as the extraordinary emoluments gained in finance, and to some extent in industry, in recent years, to which I referred at an earlier stage, may already be giving way under the pressure of a slow-down in economic activity and being brought down to more reasonable and acceptable levels. However, this still has to be seen.

The other area that will occupy a very great deal of the government's attention in its second term is Europe. I have assumed that by the time the new parliament assembles, or soon thereafter, we shall be members of the euro-zone and shall therefore have abandoned the pound for the euro. The consequence of this is that however much we may resist – this could be true of a Labour government as well as of the Conservative opposition – extensive enlargement of the area of Euroland or European Union control, much will necessarily follow from the existence of the Single Currency. The European Central Bank by 2003 will have had adequate time to get thoroughly used to its role in regulating the monetary policy for the area as a whole, and the Stability Pact and any other attempts at more co-ordinated fiscal policy, including even some elements of tax harmonization, will have begun. Britain, as a newcomer, will have to adjust itself to that situation. This means that the whole apparatus by which our present monetary policy in the first instance (and this of course includes exchange rate policy) is conducted, and also wider areas of economic management, will have to be restructured and subordinated to the operations of the central mechanisms, i.e. the Central Bank and anything else that may have been created in the meantime. (I deal with the wider possibilities in that regard in the next section.)

This will present a very difficult and complicated area of economic adjustment and management and also a contentious one. If one assumes that in the parliament after the present one the Tories will continue to show, if not a totally hostile, at any rate a highly sceptical and critical attitude towards the activities of the euro-zone, one can expect some quite difficult passages between the government and the opposition on this score.

I am assuming on this point that certainly in the next parliament the area of contention and decision-making will be confined to the immediate sequelae of the existence of a Single Currency. In the next section I have speculated how far this might go later on, but it will certainly be over by 2007. I would not have thought that this would touch on the more delicate and difficult issues of political institutions of a wider character. But even the development of some degree of quasi-political oversight of the European Central Bank – if this were to start before 2007, as I think it will – will create quite a difficult situation for the government. Much will depend on how the government handles the whole question of Economic and Monetary Union and the Single Currency between now and the end of the present parliament and the referendum, if there is to be one, on our joining the euro. On one assumption, which I am inclined to make, that almost willy-nilly the government will have to be very proactive and much more energetic in pursuing a pro-euro course before the next election, the foundation for its policy and attitude in the next parliament will have been laid. Of course, if the government were to continue on a somewhat hesitant route in this regard, and perhaps get to 2002/2003 without a very clear challenge to its opponents and to the electorate for joining the euro, we may enter the second parliament in an extremely difficult and confused stage, still outside the euro and with the monetary and general macro-economic policy of a highly uncertain and unstable character. I do not myself believe that this is a serious possibility: I think that we will in fact be full members during the next parliament and be able to participate actively and constructively, I hope, in the working out of the consequences of Economic and Monetary Union with our partners.

Five years is of course a long time and, beyond what I have just said, there will be many other issues for the government to deal with before 2007. One of the consequences of our being part of the euro-zone and of the European Union as it will then be, will be that we will have to take an active part in fashioning the European Union's position and relationship with other important economic entities outside Europe. This means first and foremost the United States, to some extent Japan – if Japan has by then recovered, as I believe it will have done, its former strength and position in the world economy – and possibly also by that time China and Russia. On the assumption I have made, this will not be a matter exclusively for our own country and for our own government. It will be a matter for the European Union, and if we have succeeded through our membership of EMU in acquiring the position within Europe that is, I think, our due and has been for far too long not realized, then we shall have a very important part to play in moulding what the European Union is going to do. It is very difficult to forecast what that might be because it depends to a large extent also on where the United States stands at that time. If the United States succeeds in continuing the extraordinary series of good economic results that it has had over almost a decade now, and thereby to demonstrate its independence of the rest of the world, then the scope for European–American relations will be relatively limited. I do not think that that is likely to be the situation. I think, as far as the United States is concerned, that even if it has what is called a soft landing from its present economic heights in the next year or two, it is unlikely to be significantly less dependent in terms of foreign trade, balance of payments, capital movements and so on, on the rest of the world economy than it has been for so long. It is even more difficult to forecast what the political configuration of the United States will be at that time, but one must hope that it will be led by people who will acknowledge its part in the world economy and be prepared to work with other major units, such as Europe, Japan etc., in creating more stable world conditions. This is a dream that is very much alive even at this stage, but has had relatively little chance of being realized, precisely because of the lack of completeness of the European Monetary and Economic Union and of the exceptional position of the United States on the one side and that of Japan on the other.

I think these circumstances will become more propitious for world-wide arrangements. If this is so, then the European Union can play a very important part in going along that road and to that end our membership could provide a vital element. At that stage our 'special relationship', of which so much has, rather unjustifiably I think, been made in the past, could become of considerable use and help create a negotiating atmosphere between the United States and Europe as well as other economic entities that I have mentioned, with a view to creating not a new Bretton Woods (the New Hampshire location of the conference in 1944 that resulted in the setting up of the World Bank and the International Monetary Fund), but something more appropriate for the world economy as it will then be.

Having said all this, I must add that it is by no means certain that much of this will come to the fore and be on the agenda before 2007. It may well not really become actual politics until the second decade, with which I deal in the next section. However, the conduct of our own government, if my assumption about its continued hold on power for a second term is proved right, could play a very important part at least in preparing the ground for further developments.

For reasons that I have set out before, I have dealt here almost exclusively with broader economico-political problems. But of course during the second quinquennium many other matters will occupy the government and will lead to legislation and other forms of action. Many of these could well be even more important than the economic and political ones that I have dealt with in fashioning the shape and character of our society. However, they are so numerous that I must refrain from trying even to mention them here, although some of them will be obvious in terms of being a continuation of efforts already made by the government in these areas of art and cultural developments generally.

To conclude Phase Two I return to the beginning and my basic assumption that Labour will be in power during this period, i.e. for a second parliament. For this assumption to become reality, the crucial question will be how the government performs between now and the election of 2002. I have already made certain remarks about that, but I want to mention at this stage one other aspect. Apart from the substantive side of its performance, the effect this will have on its own followers and on the floating voters and what responses it will evoke from the opposition, the presentation of its work is of great importance. I have already referred to the fact that the government has been very much concerned with presentation, both of its 'image' as a whole and of the reception given to its specific actions. This is nothing new and is common to all governments, but the mixture, as it were, of presentation, rhetoric or what is nowadays called 'spin-doctoring' and the reality of what is happening, varies a good deal. This government has been criticized, sometimes rightly I believe, for being unduly concerned with how the facts are presented, and the phrase 'spin-doctoring' has in fact become much more commonly used in the last two years than ever before. Leaving aside whether this accusation is justified, and if so to what extent, it will matter a great deal in the remaining three years of this government's life whether it manages to appeal to the less instructed, and perhaps less sophisticated, parts of the electorate without losing the respect and approval of its more sophisticated followers and the more sophisticated elements in the electorate at large. As the issues to which I have referred become more acute from time to time during the next three years, and the election looms nearer, it may well be that the government will decide that *mutatis mutandis* a touch of the wartime 'blood, sweat and tears' would not come amiss and might in fact be more telling and attractive to the electorate than a more glossy and more euphemistic presentation with its appearance of self-satisfaction. If this were to be the case, it must not be overdone and it is unlikely to be. Politicians are not preachers and should not be. They are not moralists and they should not be. The balance between natural appearance and appeal to basic instincts, and trust in the electorate's good sense in distinguishing between good performance and bad, is not easy. But I do believe that this is an aspect that, when the election comes, the government will very much have to bear in mind, but I also believe that this is not something that can be summoned up during the last month or two before the election and the actual campaign, but must be carefully prepared. Three years is by no means too long for this purpose.

The Second Decade

Up to the year 2007 – that is to say, to the end of the present parliament and the next one – it is risky, but just about possible, to forecast what will happen. I am of course making the basic assumption that both these parliaments run their full course of about five years each. After that, for the decade from 2007 onwards, it becomes easier for the simple reason that from that point on forecasting in the strict sense is hardly possible. It then gives way to speculation on very broad trends that are likely to affect the fortunes of our country. This may be daring, but it is at the same time more of a 'free for all'.

I have assumed in what has gone before that up to 2007 we shall have a government roughly of the present kind, that is to say New Labour, if that label persists. It will be composed of more or less the same political elements of which it now consists. Obviously there is no particular point in speculating about individuals. Actuarially, as well as in terms of his political power, it is reasonable to assume that the party will be led by Mr Blair and that he will therefore remain Prime Minister up to 2007. It does not really much matter what other significant figures there will be in the government, particularly in the parliament after the present one. It does not really affect, in prospect at least, the course of events. Events themselves will be influenced, perhaps determined, by individuals: by the principal actors in the government as well as by leading figures in trade, industry, finance, in the arts and by so-called opinion-formers, journalists and broadcasters, to say nothing of scientists and technologists. So we can simply ignore the composition of the leading actors for that period. This is what I have done, with the exception of assuming the continued leadership of Mr Blair. We may also assume that political attachments will continue, although the case is certainly no longer as it was over a hundred years ago when Gilbert could assert that 'every little boy or girl that is born into this world alive is either a little Liberal or else a little Conservative'. At that time of course Labour did not count.

The doctrinal differences of political parties (as is the case in some respects between the Republicans and the Democrats in the United States) have paled a great deal. Nevertheless, the main parties still maintain a core of adherents who will vote for them more or less in all circumstances. We certainly have people who will vote Labour whatever happens and who would never vote Tory, and similarly the other way round. (I leave the Liberal Democrats out of account.) They identify themselves with these parties in all sorts of ways. Much of it may date back to earlier times when these parties were much more distinguishable by their political philosophies. Some of it may be family tradition, what 'Pa' or 'Ma' used to support and used to vote for. Also, there is no doubt that despite the disappearance of 'class' as far as Labour and almost equally so as far as the Tories are concerned – at any rate for specific political purposes – there is nevertheless still a residue of feeling that identifies some sections of the population, not always characterized by income or status, but often so, and that makes them adherents of this party or of that.

When it comes to what happens after 2007, the difficulty lies more in choosing what are likely to be more transcendental currents both of evolution and of more radical change that will mould the character of the body politic of our nation and will affect the position of our country as a constituent element in the world geopolitical structure.

I begin with one that I regard as absolutely overriding, namely the international position of the UK. This has undergone very considerable changes in the last hundred years. There is no doubt in my mind that as the new millennium gets under way, this will continue to be a crucial problem to which we will have to find either a solution or an accommodation. The last hundred years have been characterized by a relative decline in the position of Britain in the world. Even the most ardent believer in our continued greatness cannot help noting that the great characteristics of the nineteenth century, *Pax Britannica* and what I would like to call the *Aequilibrium Britannicum*, dominated the scene not only of the developed world but to a large extent of the known world as a whole. *Pax Britannica* was guaranteed by the British Navy; *Aequilibrium Britannicum* was guaranteed by the central position of sterling as a world currency and of the British monetary authorities, first and foremost the Bank of England, as the managers of that currency. The Governor's eyebrows traditionally dominated the banking scene at home. The action of the Bank of England went far beyond that. The Gold Standard, whatever adjustment it suffered during the nineteenth century, was essentially dominated by the bank rate and by the credit policy of the Bank of England, which determined by way of the 'specie points' – the points at which gold came in or went out of the country – what the exchange rates would be and with it what the monetary conditions in the different countries would have to be.

This situation ended with the First World War. Apart from all the other consequences that it had on international power relations and on the economic and industrial structure of our country, it certainly shattered these two pillars of British pre-eminence. Of course, Britain was on the winning side in the war. This was achieved by 'bringing in the new world to redress the balance of the old', as at a later stage one great British statesman was so rightly to point out. Without the intervention of the United States, the First World War could not have been won by the Allies and the domination, beginning with the Continent, by Germany prevented. This change in the relative position of Europe vis-à-vis the United States and of the United Kingdom as the most powerful country in Europe has been still further consolidated during the Second World War where the intervention of the United States was absolutely critical for defeating Hitler's dominating ambitions, quite apart from the dreadful threat of the 'loss of freedom' to Britain, which might have engulfed the whole of Europe.

The domination of the United States was not absolute. Anyone who actively and objectively examined the situation had to recognize that the Strategic Air Force rather than the British Navy was now guaranteeing the *Pax Americana* and also that the *Aequilibrium Britannicum* had been replaced by an *Aequilibrium Americanum* dominated by the dollar managed by the American monetary authorities. That domination was hemmed in by various postwar devices and institutions. There had been created a far more ambitious and a far more effective and powerful instrument than the League of Nations after the First World War, to which America did not belong, namely the United Nations. Furthermore, partly as a result of the genius of Keynes, in 1944 Bretton Woods instituted a regime for both reconstruction and development as well as for the regulation of monetary conditions. This also provided a mechanism for American power, but at the same time a brake on total American domination.

The other institution planned at Bretton Woods, the International Trade Organization (ITO), had to be replaced by the GATT, the General Agreement on Tariffs and Trade, which only many years later was turned into a World Trade Organization owing to Congressional opposition to the original proposal.

At the same time, apart from these world-wide constructions into which Britain fitted, the European Integration movement, which had its roots deep in the early years of the century, even starting in the latter part of the last century, and which gained considerable ground as a result of the wartime Hitlerian domination of the Continent of Europe, took wings and as a result of the work of Jean Monnet became a fact through the creation first of the Common Market, later the European Economic Community. Britain took a long time to make up its mind to join, but eventually did in 1972 and is a member of what is now called the European Union. This, together with the Bretton Woods institution, purports to represent, and to some degree actually does, a kind of world system that has taken the place of the old British domination, and later to a significant measure American domination, of the world strategic, political, and economic scene.

Britain has accommodated itself more or less to these vast

changes. The Empire has disappeared, the Commonwealth has taken its place and although it still has some reality, it is far from being a major, effective, world-wide factor in determining political and economic evolution.

Britain was supposed to stand in the middle of three circles, the American, the Commonwealth and the European. That was a total illusion. It was an adequate description of the dilemma in which we found ourselves, but it was certainly an illusion if it was meant to represent a really effective source of power and influence. No definitive resolution of this problem has been found and in a way has not really been attempted. And that was probably right for a long time. I would say that the ten years from 2007 onwards are likely to be dominated by an increasing pressure to find for our country a more lasting, and a more effective position in this kaleidoscope of world power.

Why should this be so? What I have described, if it is reasonably accurate, is a secular trend, the kind that in this case has lasted a century, but in other cases of historic change, of the decline of empires, even modern ones such as the Dutch, the Spanish and the Portuguese, has taken longer still. Could it not be that we shall go on in much the same way as we have done, say, since the end of the war, playing as best we can a role based on our considerable remaining strength, material, moral and political, and avoiding any more pointed solution of this problem? I think myself that this is not impossible, but it is less likely than the alternative, namely that we shall be under increasing pressure to make a more definite choice. This is partly due to an increasing tendency all over the world towards regionalization. It has not perhaps been very effective so far and of course it is of different characters. NAFTA is very special. It is essentially, although this would not be admitted by some of its members, a means of spreading American influence while at the same time making it more palatable through the inclusion of influences from elsewhere, Mexico and Canada particularly. There are, however, others. In South-East Asia there are attempts towards some kind of regional economic and perhaps even political construction. In Latin

America there is no great evidence of this yet and it is not at all certain that a different tendency of an important character towards regionalization will emerge there in the next ten or fifteen years, although it cannot be excluded.

But as far as the United Kingdom is concerned, by far the most important factor that leads one to the view that more definite decisions may have to be made over the ten years from 2007 onwards is Europe. Europe is already a thorn in our side and an impediment to our so obvious and so understandable desire to have a quieter life. Many would prefer not to be forced into making decisions of this character, to live as happily as we can and to use our influence as best we can all over the world, leaning more in one direction rather than another from time to time as circumstances and our own interest demand. The progress of European integration has practically destroyed that possibility. It is already the major problem of this particular kind that motivates political activity, opinion at large, vigorous intellectual debate – and indeed considerably influences the international activities of our government. In itself, it is likely to become the dominant political problem of the next eight years or so, that is to say during this parliament and the next. Looking beyond, it is also likely both in the short term and (in so far as it is not resolved) in the longer term, to influence our broader world political posture. It is true that in many respects we have both interests and assets, as well as commitments, outside Europe often of a more significant character than is the case of our partners in the European Union, not even excluding France, which is at present internationally the most important of the other members of the Union. Our commitments stem partly from our role in the last war, from the remaining world-wide economic and strategic power that we possess, including above all the nuclear power and the close relationship in its development and use with the United States. Our participation and experience of armed conflicts in various parts of the world since the end of the Second World War, whatever one may think about it, has certainly given us a status in these matters that other European countries do not possess.

We have still considerable economic assets, not so much in our traditional strength of manufacturing and exporting industries, which have declined a great deal in recent years, but certainly in international financial arrangements where the City still plays a part, which is in many respects equal to, and in some even greater than, that of New York. It is certainly in a different class from that of Paris, Milan, Amsterdam or Frankfurt, although, as I have indicated elsewhere, with the progress of the euro and the development of the European Central Bank in Frankfurt, there will be in the middle and long term a shift of the centre of gravity away from London that we must carefully monitor as it proceeds. Our cultural influence is enormous, not so much in regard to our achievements in literature and the arts, great though these are, but as a result of our language. It is the language that was the vehicle of the greatest poet of modern times, quite apart from the fact that English is by now well established as the universal language of communication not only in business but in a host of other respects. French may continue to be a very important language in formal diplomatic relationships. German may still have some special status in Central and Eastern Europe, particularly in the areas that were part of the Austro-Hungarian monarchy – though this is actually much less evident than one might have expected. Spanish continues of course to be extremely important because of Latin America, though even here English has penetrated to a very considerable extent. This is certainly true of Asia where as of now no other really universal *lingua franca* has emerged.

Despite these very considerable assets, which we have perhaps not used in the best possible way to secure an effective and solidly based position for ourselves, we need to decide more closely in which group in the increasingly structured world power map we want to put our major weight. I believe that this must inevitably be Europe and that it is very much in our interest to do so soon and unequivocally. Looking beyond Europe, we must ensure that the Europe to which we must increasingly belong, is a powerful and effective instrument in world politics in the decades to come in the pursuit of peace and prosperity.

So even if, as I assume, we have joined EMU and are playing our part in the development of the European Union as a whole, also gradually embracing (as and when they join) the countries that are at the moment in the ante-chamber as candidates, we shall not be through with this process by 2007. From then on, as members, we shall have to consider very carefully with those of our partners who are playing a major role in the European Union as it will then be what will be most effective in assuring for Europe the right sort of position in whatever constellation of world power has by then developed.

In what I say above, I have not specially stressed foreign policy and defence issues, because it is already plain that these will exert an even more acute influence than the longer-term economic and financial ones. Already attitudes to the problems of the Middle East have sharpened the choice between Europe and the United States with armed conflicts presenting alternatives that cannot be ignored. This is also true of the continuing discussion on defence arrangements concerning the Western European Union and NATO; and perhaps most significant of all, the difficult and as yet unresolved problems of intra-European and transatlantic arrangements in the defence and related industries.

The Internal Problems

I begin with some internal problems, although even 'internal' problems, that is to say, problems that can be distinguished from the broader international considerations with which I have just dealt, are affected by them, as I shall show later. Foremost among these will be two: first, the structure of the mechanics and the guiding lines of macro-economic policy; second, the resolution of the problem of poverty and what I believe will then still be the very large discrepancy between rich and poor. Both will be crucial testing grounds for the structure of our political parties and for the contents of their principles and programmes.

Before considering these, a few words are appropriate on more general aspects that are not directly economic.

Of my twenty-year period – that is to say, over the next eighteen years or so from the time of writing this – it is reasonable to suppose that many important changes, perhaps some crucial changes, will have taken place or will be about to take place in the broad socio-political framework in which our country is situated. There are a number of constitutional changes already pending and in addition to these there will be many not directly constitutional but still fundamental since they will affect the general operating environment.

As far as constitutional changes are concerned, the most important have already in principle taken place and are now in the process of implementation. These are the degree of autonomy in the government of Scotland, and to a lesser degree in Wales, by the creation of a Scottish Parliament and a Welsh Assembly. There will be executives in both cases, but the whole question of the relationship of the executives to the elected institutions and in turn to the Westminster Parliament and to the Westminster

Government, have been matters of considerable controversy while the legislation has been going through parliament. While this will obviously be resolved in one way or another before the end of the first decade, as I have called it, I am nevertheless mentioning it here because the wider and longer-term consequences of this degree of devolution will go on for some considerable time. The change, although novel as far as the history of the United Kingdom in recent centuries is concerned, is historically of course by no means entirely unprecedented and the arguments that have taken place, both about the scope of this change and about the precise modalities by which it is implemented, have not reflected any kind of archaic reference to older forms of constitutional arrangements within the British Isles.

I say that the consequences will continue for some considerable time because, although the powers of the parliament in Scotland and of the assembly in Wales and of their respective executives will clearly have been defined before the end of 2007, nevertheless the way they work out in practice will plainly give rise to continued argument and controversy. In one way or another they will affect policy issues, particularly to the extent to which they should affect the taxing powers of the two countries – at the moment quite limited even in the case of Scotland.

There is no doubt that the House of Lords will have been reformed before the end of the parliament after the present one and perhaps even before its beginning. It is not absolutely necessary, but certainly may happen – and in the opinion of some, which I share, is desirable – that the reform of the House of Lords should lead to a change in the administration of justice at the highest level. In theory, since nomination will continue to be one way of creating members of the Upper House, it is quite feasible for the present category of Law Lords to continue. This is in fact what the government has stipulated (including the elevation of bishops). Sooner or later, however, I believe that this will cease to be the case and that a proper supreme court of justice will be established. In this respect at any rate, there is no good reason why the present combination of power – the legislature and the judiciary – should be preserved, even if it is in regard to the legislative and the executive.

Electoral reform, although it seems to be marking time at the moment, will probably also have taken place. It is not possible to say exactly what form it will have taken since both the major political parties are at best uncertain, and at worst actually hostile, as to the idea of departing from the 'first past the post' system. Only the Liberal Democrats are for obvious reasons in favour of introducing an element, perhaps a large element, of the list system, but it is pretty certain that some kind of electoral reform will have taken place by the end of the period under review. Needless to say, it is not possible to guess now what the effect on the operation of our political democracy will be as a result of these changes. Many people who are doubtful about the list system, and about any kind of proportional representation, fear that it will give rise to a multiplication of political parties and, therefore, to the possibility of less stable governments than the ones that the 'first past the post' system has traditionally produced in our country for centuries. Beyond that, however, there is a further question that has been raised by some political philosophers, particularly on the left, in recent months, namely the question of the whole future of the 'majority democracy' under which we have been living for so long. It is difficult to pinpoint precisely the reasons for this doubt that has arisen, but it lies to some extent at least in the observed strategy and tactics of the present government, and more particularly of the present Prime Minister, Mr Blair. It can be taken for granted by what he has said and done before the election, and certainly since coming into power, that he is most anxious to establish the present government and any regime over which he presides, as being a government of all the people for all the people and not merely a government of one particular party. The very label 'New Labour' suggests as much, although it is obviously also designed to make that party more eligible than it was before 1997. If he succeeds and a general discontent, or at least neutralism, towards party labels, which seems to exist particularly among the younger electorate, gains ground, it could lead to some recasting of the political map away from party allegiance at all costs. The blurring of the basic differences between the two main parties, and indeed between Conservatives, Labour and Liberal Democrats alike – despite the fact that on occasions and for some less fundamental issues the party battle is still as fierce as ever – also lends colour to the view that the future pattern of our political life, quite apart from the effects of electoral reform, will be less party-dominated than before.

Another area of great change that has already been started by the present government and will undoubtedly continue throughout the next decade or two is the justice system – that is to say, not only the justice system as regards crime and civil matters as such, but the questions of the objectives of justice, of punishment for different types of misdemeanour and felonies, of methods of law enforcement and the role of the police, particularly given the specific problems that have beset some police forces, not least the Metropolitan force, of preservation of standards and avoidance of corruption. All these are already very much in hand and have occupied parliamentary time during the government's first eighteen months. While it is quite impossible to foresee what exactly the picture will be in 2017, say, it will almost certainly be very different from what we have today.

Education is another great area that will have changed. There have been many changes since the end of the War and others are already taking place now. I am speaking here of change of substance, as well as of organization and administration, quite apart from the question of how education at all its levels should be funded. This last point is the one that most obviously and most often occupies political debate, including parliamentary time, but quite apart from that the structure of our educational system and its content and the objectives to be aimed at will certainly be re-examined and will be different at the end of the period from what they are now. Among the many issues that will have to be tackled, if not resolved, is the relationship between education in the old broad sense of the word and vocational instruction and training at various stages of the citizen's life. The question of the relationship between basic research carried out by the higher institutes of learning and the needs and interests of business in the results of research and their application for practical purposes is by no means yet entirely clear or entirely resolved. At the moment the issue is somewhat in the background and the one-time burning question of the 'purity' of the academic researcher for new scientific truths and new technological possibilities has abated. Universities are only too happy to accept even fairly closely earmarked funds for particular purposes, many of which are then, to some extent at least, directly or indirectly available for the more mundane purposes of business. I am not sure that this situation will remain as it is and it may well be that once more the question of the relationship between academia and the market place will become acute.

Health will of course be a very important subject from an economic point of view and I shall refer to that again presently, but quite apart from that, the whole question of principles to guide the maintenance, preservation and securing of the citizen's health and his expectation of life is undergoing substantial changes as a result again of scientific progress both in medicine and in surgical procedures. The extent to which these influence the more mundane problems of government in regard to the funding of health care is already evident because of the greater availability of drugs and other medicines, the greater availability of highly sophisticated surgical procedures and the greater expectation of life, which has changed the age structure of the population and also, therefore, the burden of maintaining people in health.

All these areas are of very great importance and it may well be that well beyond the more day-to-day problems of fiscal and monetary policy, of how to secure growth and employment and how to relate to our compatriots as well as to people outside, these will prove to be even more important. But they fall outside the broad economic theme that I have laid down for this particular study and therefore, beyond mentioning them and indicating their all-important impact on the rest of our lives, I must go on to these other matters.

Of the areas within which I have grouped what I have to say in this Part I have already dealt with the broad question, i.e. the position of our country in the world. After a mention of major questions – constitutional and otherwise – that are not directly economic issues, I now return to these. The first question is what the economic objectives should be and what are the methods, institutions and practices for trying to meet them. The other question is what to do about the continuing disparity of wealth and income and the persistence of poverty.

I have already dealt with the question of the present government's attitude and programme in regard to social policy so-called. I do not believe that as things look at the moment we are likely to have solved this problem. We may, however, have dealt with it, at least to the extent that it will not threaten to become an acute issue in this parliament or in the next. This is why I believe that it will still be very much with us and if other things have been satisfactorily dealt with, it will not be possible to avoid dealing with it from 2007 onwards. This problem raises some extremely difficult issues both intellectual and in terms of practical politics. We have not yet reached the stage – and I do not think we shall reach it in 2007 – when, paraphrasing Abraham Lincoln, we may say, 'This nation will not long endure, half poor and half rich.' That is not the situation and I do not think it is very likely that it would come to that in the next few years. On the other hand, I do not believe that any significant diminution of the inequalities that exist now will have taken place. Inequality and redistributive measures, such as a combination of taxation and benefits, present intellectual, political and practical administrative problems of great difficulty. Sooner or later, however, possibly even through the pressure from Europe, which may well have to deal with this issue also, particularly after the enlargement that will have taken place by then (even leaving Russia out of account), this will become a matter of priority. If by then the macro-economic management of our own country and of Europe as a whole has been effective, if growth and employment have been put on an upward path and are reasonably encouraging, tackling the problem of inequality should become easier. Indeed all problems of that character are easier when you are in a growth situation and not plagued by large-scale unemployment.

As regards macro-economic management, this is even more difficult to deal with, not only because it is not at all clear how far by 2007 this will be a matter for national governments, including our own, and how far it will have become a matter for the European Union or at least for those countries who have by that time joined Economic and Monetary Union. But even apart from that as it were technical and structural issue, there is a more fundamental one. As of now, it is by no means clear what the correct macro-economic objectives and policy should be – leaving aside the broadest, which, like motherhood and sliced bread, everybody subscribes to, namely economic growth and employment. Nor is it clear what are the right means for reaching these objectives, nor what are the right institutional arrangements for exercising these means of policy. I have already dealt at some length with this problem in considering the issues that face our government here and now and over the next few years. It is of course possible that analytical research and careful examination of data may by 2007 have produced a system covering these various aspects I have described that holds out the hope of more effective conduct and control of the economy in order to secure growth, rising standards of living and sustained employment with only frictional or technological fluctuations. The history in this regard is not encouraging, partly because some of the innovative ideas that have sprung up from time to time – Keynes and his gigantic leap forward in these matters is an example – have been greeted with considerable objections and resistance, sometimes without any clear intellectual foundation, but nevertheless effective politically.

Another group of problems that will preoccupy us in the ten years with which I am dealing concerns the economy in its concrete manifestations. What are going to be the principal economic activities of the country both in the real economy and in the financial field? What will be the role of private enterprise as against state enterprise (if any is left)? What will be the scope of state regulation of aspects of the economy? What will be the corporate structure that will predominate; will it be largely national or international? How far will the process of globalizing enterprise have progressed at that time? These are the main questions that arise outside of, but not unconnected with, the activities of government. As in the case of the other areas of this enquiry, this one too is going to be affected by the broader framework of national and international socio-political structure.

I believe that these two areas of policy can be treated separately from the broader questions of our international relationships. This is particularly in relation to our membership of EMU, as I am convinced it will then be, whatever scope of European integration may have been reached. I do not believe, however, that it will have reached that stage where a considerable degree of individual national member action in certain economic and social fields is impossible. Nevertheless, now that the euro has come into being and has been accompanied by various statements of ambitions or expectations on the Continent, it is difficult to believe that over the next eighteen years or so there will not be a further diminution of national freedom of action in these matters. However, despite my own clearly stated preference for our full participation in European integration, I do not believe that that process will have led to anything like a federal system of government for Europe by the year 2017 or even over the next decade. Much, as I have already indicated, will have been accomplished even in areas of defence policy and foreign affairs quite apart from those flowing directly from the Single Market and the Single Currency, such as in some areas of taxation. However, I do not think that the process will have reached a point where we can speak of federal law having a considerable sway over the activities of government, including member governments themselves. The only factors that might change that outlook would be quite unforeseeable and revolutionary developments, possibly stemming from outside. One cannot entirely rule out such developments, for example in regard to nuclear power and possibly nuclear weaponry. However, I doubt whether these, whether they occur across the Atlantic or in Russia or anywhere else, will in the timespan under review be of such a character and size as to influence the economic issues that I am here concerned with.

Of course, what is happening on the Union level in Europe will undoubtedly affect my two areas of study, namely macro-economic policy in its objectives, its methods and its instruments, and the broader social policy that has an effect on the distribution of wealth and income and on the general social structuring of the populations of our countries. In regard to macro-economic policy I shall deal with that shortly in some more detail because there are certain things that may be expected to flow from the Single Market and the Single Currency, which some will read with pleasure while others will reject and detest them. Similarly in regard to the broader aspects of social policy, there are already various provisions in the Maastricht Treaty, to which the members of the European Union are subject. There will certainly be others that will perhaps apply more specifically to those who are members of the Economic and Monetary Union only and affect working conditions, minimum wages, trade union recognition etc., which sooner or later will have an impact on the distribution of wealth and income. Macro-economic policy will also be a factor if – and this is perhaps a big if – it gets into the subject of taxation, and by that I mean not only the more obvious removals of discriminatory practices designed to affect competitiveness between one member of the Union against another, but questions that go further in regard to personal taxation, both income and capital. If these were to take place, although this is highly doubtful still, then obviously they would also have an impact on the distribution of wealth and on poverty etc.

As I have already said, these broader issues of the long-term future of the European Union are already beginning to agitate the political scene in this country. On the birth of the euro this is not surprising, and people are beginning to line up, some in a quite surprising way, for and against what they consider to be the future federal unified state that the advocates of the euro and its promoters are intent upon creating. I doubt whether this present agitation will continue at this pace for very long. It is, however, likely to re-emerge from time to time, including, as I have indicated in the previous section, at the time of the 2002 election if Britain has not taken a decision before then, and certainly after that, and will form without a doubt the major issue between the two major political parties. What I think those who have been in favour of the Single Currency, and continue to advocate our joining it, will have to consider very carefully, certainly in the next ten to fifteen years, is what exactly the shape of the European Union, including the Single Currency area and probably including a number of countries not yet members, will really have to be as a political entity. If I am right in thinking that it will not go as far as creating a real federal state, what are the alternatives that are open to it? To what extent will the increasing economic integration, and what I believe to be inevitably also the increasing united action in the field of foreign policy and defence, affect institutions in regard to decisions that have hitherto been the preserve of the nation state? It is pointless to speculate too much about this at this stage because the formation of opinion in these matters, the emergence of new ideas, the search for precedence in past history and in other political entities existing in the world today, may well produce quite unimagined solutions to this problem. For my part, all I would say – and perhaps I am repeating what I have already said – is that I do not believe we shall reach anything like the structure of the United States of America in Europe by the end of the period that I am reviewing, that is to say by 2017 to 2020. None of the preconditions that favoured the creation of the United States as a federation rather than as a totally centralized political unit exist in Europe and even the advance of integration in the fields I have mentioned is unlikely to produce them.

Whatever may have been the innermost motives of founders of the Common Market, notably Jean Monnet – and I believe that

he certainly had it in mind that at some point in the future
something like the United States of Europe would emerge – the
not only overt but also certainly inner driving force of integration
up to now has been economic. The recent addition of foreign
affairs and defence has largely been caused by events that are not
inherent in the process of European integration. They have been
brought about by the fall of the Soviet regime, the disappearance
of the Berlin Wall, the unification of Germany, the rethinking
about the role of NATO and of the Western European Union in
regard to defence. Added to these have been the increasing pressures on European countries, particularly those belonging to the
European Union, to act in trouble spots like Yugoslavia (Bosnia
and Kosovo) and so on. In other words, they have not been
inherent in the process of creating a European integration on the
economic front. They have been extraneous and, although
powerful enough to create pressure for immediate collective
action, cannot in my view be regarded as inevitably pointing
towards political unification as well.

Nevertheless, I would not deny that even the progress of economic union, which I believe will proceed faster than it has in
the past and will include this country, will inevitably create the
need of some degree of common action that is normally the preserve of the single state. This may start particularly with taxation,
although it must be noted here that the main impetus for greater
integration has come from the need to protect the achievements
of economic union and more particularly the Single Market. That
is to say they have come from the need to ensure that there are
not factors still operating in the individual member countries that
would falsify, or perhaps even frustrate, what is aimed at in
the Single Market and what is going to be strengthened by the
existence of the Single Currency. In other words, the phrase 'level
playing field' has been used again and again to justify the attempt
to produce more integration in one field or another so as to ensure
that the Single Market can work properly. Now this is clearly a
very debatable area, and particularly in regard to matters like
taxation it is certainly possible to draw a distinction between those

aspects of taxation – and spending too for that matter – that are obviously anti-Single Market (in the sense that they lead to a privileged competitive position for enterprises in one member country as against the others) and those that really have no direct bearing on this particular issue. The opponents of our joining the Single Currency will of course not accept that there is this distinction and have already made very antagonistic responses to some of the suggestions coming from across the Channel, particularly from Germany, and to some extent also from France, that some areas of taxation might need to be examined to see if a degree of harmonization, perhaps in the sense of the prohibition of certain practices, might be appropriate. It would to my mind be unwise and very hard to justify in any event for Britain to take this line too strongly. It is perfectly in order to insist on drawing the distinction that I have made above between different types of taxation and their influence on the working of the rest of European integration, but simply to oppose any kind of examination of taxation by members of the European Union as a whole, even if they are not confined only to those that belong to the euro-zone, as I think it could reasonably be argued, is perfectly legitimate.

There are other areas that indeed have to some extent already been experimented with in the way of harmonization of unification. The large number of the directives of the European Union, to most of which we have subscribed, are concerned with such matters. These relate for example to qualifications for exercising certain professions and the extent to which these are harmonized. This will obviously have some influence on the education leading up to the acquisition of qualifications of this kind; but this is a very slow, long and indirect process. That perhaps eventually the exercise of the medical profession will be more or less on an equal footing, and that acquiring a qualification in one member country will also bring with it the right to exercise that profession in another, is by no means unlikely and is to some extent already in force. This may eventually also apply to others. For example, given globalization, the accountancy profession in any event will be increasingly harmonized, not only within the European Union, but probably on a world scale as between the more advanced industrialized countries. Similarly, the movements of capital and the greater use of multiple stock exchange listings for major companies all over the world, certainly on the European stock exchanges, will produce a greater degree of uniformity in listing requirements, in accountability, in reporting requirements and all that goes with that. I do not see why these matters should in any way exercise the minds of even the most formidable defenders of national sovereignty. As in all these matters, however, a line must be drawn here and there. As far as education in the broadest sense is concerned, I see no reason why this should be subject to any great degree of harmonization except that which will take place spontaneously in regard to vocational training and education – in other words, that which will be brought about by the need to have people who can, if they wish, move from one part of the Union to another and have the necessary qualifications to do so. But this is not necessarily imposed by the government, although there may be areas where government action could legitimately be exercised. As far as health and health services are concerned, the degree of harmonization between different countries is to my mind not very great if it is to be based on state prescriptive action. It is said that already today the availability of health services of different degrees and with different ease of access in different countries of the Union is causing a certain amount of migration of people in need of health care from one country to another. It is by no means proved that this is a major factor at all and when one considers the natural obstacles, so to speak, in the way of full migration, this seems to me pretty obvious. Certainly – particularly in exceptional cases and depending also on the question of whether such movements can be funded or not – it is already possible for some private patients, or even for some health service patients, to receive exceptional treatment where this is available only in one particular part of the world, and this of course goes way beyond the countries of the Union. It affects particularly the United States in the sense that very often certain special treatment by drugs not available elsewhere, or by surgical procedures not developed to the same extent elsewhere, are sought in the United States, but it is only in very rare cases where this can be obtained by people who are not in a position to finance this kind of service themselves.

The administration of justice certainly, except in the very carefully prescribed cases that directly affect the working of economic integration, is clearly not going to have much effect, except by example and imitation. There is no need to object, for example, to some innovation that has taken place, say, in Germany, or for that matter in the United States, being experimented with and eventually applied in our country, and vice-versa, but I do not see any movement for any great harmonization of criminal justice except in special cases of law enforcement and co-operation between police forces, which is already very much in hand and will continue to a large extent in any event, whatever happens within the European Union.

I do not propose to go through every single aspect of national state activity today that may become a subject of debate and controversy in regard to its possible harmonization on a European Union level and, as I have said again and again, which very often also applies way beyond the European Union. I think the examples I have given demonstrate sufficiently that there is nothing inherent in what is going on now in regard to the euro and its sequelae that inevitably leads to the creation of a total federal system of government.

More about this in the next chapter.

The Political Landscape

For this, the final chapter of this book, I have chosen a particularly hazardous speculation of what might be the situation by the end of the second decade. I have called it 'The Political Landscape'. By that I mean the structure, position, programmes and intentions of the political parties. The first question to be answered is why this should be a subject of speculation. The political landscape of this country has undergone many changes, particularly in the last 200 years, but in many basic respects it has remained unaltered in the current century. This political landscape, however, as it stands in the last year of the twentieth century, and of the second millennium, shows some signs that it will be subject to potentially considerable changes over the next decade or two. The main reason for this is that the change that occurred in 1997, when Labour was elected after eighteen years in the wilderness, may well turn out to have been something of a seismic change in the composition of our political structure.

It is by no means clear, as I have already said at an earlier stage in this book, to what extent the victory of Labour and the unprecedented size of that victory were due to its own merits and to its own appeal to the electors and how far it was, as is so often the case in our political system, a failure of the government in power to maintain the affection and approval of the electorate. Many people believe that the Conservative Party had in fact come to the end of its hold over the electorate in 1992 and that their defeat was only delayed for five years largely by the fact that Labour was still not regarded by enough of the electorate as capable of taking over the country and leading it forward in a manner acceptable to the electorate. The outcome was, no doubt, a mixture of the two, but in any event the transformation of Labour from 'old' to 'New' has had something to do with what happened. In any event, whether it did or not, Labour – New Labour – is now in power and, as I have indicated at a number of points, will almost certainly remain in power for the next parliament. However, I have also indicated that whatever may be the specific programme and plans of the present government, or the absence of such specific plans, for which they are from time to time criticized, they have certainly, as far as the leadership is concerned (and particularly the Prime Minister), laid out an ambitious intention of transforming the political landscape. One can almost apply to them the phrase that four prominent Labour leaders used in the eighties when they broke away from the Labour Party and when three of them finally came to rest in the Liberal Democratic Party, i.e. 'to break the mould of politics'. This ambition, perhaps not very clearly enunciated as yet, consists in getting away from the implications of majority rule, i.e. of the winning party representing, as it were, a section of the electorate only, whether this is 'class' in the old-fashioned sense of the word or not, but at any rate, only a section of the electorate, rather than the people as a whole – a very ambitious desire, but one that the Prime Minister has hinted at from time to time, much beyond the almost ritual assurance by most prime ministers on taking office that they will govern on behalf of all the people.

Most recently he has in fact put a little more flesh on the bones of this ambition in a speech in which he forecast that after not very many years from now, we shall all be 'middle class' – in other words, that the distinctions that have hitherto marked out different bits of the electorate and have, therefore, led to different political parties focusing their appeal in a specific way to attract specific bits of the electorate, has gone by the board, and that the electorate will be so uniform – homogeneous perhaps – that to succeed a political party will have not only to declare but also to prove that it represents the electorate as a whole.

The idea that we are all on the way to becoming middle class has some arguments in its favour. Certainly in terms of lifestyle, the distinctions do not wholly represent differences of status or even differences of wealth and income as they have done traditionally for so long. A substantial section of the population either already possesses, or certainly has the desire and ambition to possess, a lifestyle that can be fairly defined as that of the middle class, or perhaps one should say now the middle middle class. Differences of lifestyle have, of course, by no means disappeared; and what is more important, if we are really to be all middle class as far as lifestyle is concerned, it is essential that the differences in wealth and income that exist at the moment, and that to a large extent still determine lifestyle, should be much diminished, if not altogether removed.

Whether this can, let alone will, in fact happen over the next 17/18 years or so, is highly debatable. Certainly as far as the government's policy in its first two years of office is concerned, I have already said that very little has been done in that direction, and certainly, explicitly at least, any desire by redistributive taxation to reduce these differences of wealth and income do not seem to be at all in favour with the Labour leadership. They could of course argue that they are trying to arrive at something similar by other means: the 'welfare to work' scheme, the specific changes in the welfare provision and other benefits, the substantial changes in the health service and in education, which to a large extent determine the standard of living of the mass of the population and others. These, it may be argued, are designed, explicitly or in their eventual outcome, not so much to remove differences of income and wealth, but to make them less relevant to the actual standard of living enjoyed by the population. However, this I think is not really an adequate answer to the question and it remains to be seen whether the government while it is in power will in fact bring in measures of a specifically redistributive character to underpin, if that is their intention, their conviction that we are all moving to a middle-middle-class style of life and status in the community.

It would be a very long and difficult way to go. Already now, as I have indicated, the disagreements within the party of the government, although not yet of an acute character and certainly not 'life-threatening', are beginning to appear and with a parliamentary majority of the kind they have, as I have emphasized again and again, the danger of fissiparous tendencies appearing and 'old' Labour raising its head again is not negligible. Some of the recent more personal (and to that extent not directly relevant) difficulties that some of the ministers who have for the moment left the government have got into indicate that, whether this applies to the electorate as a whole or not, certainly within the party itself there is a strong residue of beliefs, not to say principles, that can be challenged only at considerable risk. These derive to a large extent from the whole mode of thinking, the mind-set, of old Labour rather than of New Labour.

One may give to the government all the credit for sincerity that one likes, and I am quite prepared to do so myself and believe that they are genuinely convinced that the measures they are about to introduce will over time in fact produce that more egalitarian society that is desirable – even if it is not defined in the same way as it would have been defined by old Labour. But that takes time and whether the contrary tendencies within the party in particular, but also in the electorate in general, will be slow enough before they come to the surface to allow this time to be used appropriately and to produce the desired results is not assured.

Still, let us assume that the idea of creating a middle-middle-class society – or at least of not impeding the tendencies in that direction that are already operating, and also of underpinning it with suitable economic reforms – proceeds and is reasonably successful by the end of my period under review. We would then have one party, which at any rate has held power for half that period and possibly for longer than that, that is devoted to that particular vision of society and determined to create and maintain it and continue to be in power on that basis. What in that case is the new political landscape going to be like?

I leave the Liberal Democrats for the moment, partly because it is difficult to see what their role could be, before looking at the major opposition party that governed the country for so many years in the last half-century. I proceed therefore, to examine the potential of the Tories over the remaining part of the two decades. This presents even more difficulties than with Labour because the Tories suffered an enormous defeat in 1997, and as far as one can see at this stage, are still in considerable disarray. The leader seems to have consolidated his position somewhat, but on the other hand the disagreements with the old 'grandees' of the party – and by that I do not mean only the grandees in the sense of status but grandees in the sense of long service to the party and considerable position of authority before Mr Hague became party leader – are still very marked even though the Tory Party, as always, is rather more adept than Labour in hiding internal differences or at least ensuring that they do not fester openly.

For the next election, if not beyond, it is not easy to see what could be the major – I emphasize major – issues on which the Tory Party might carve out for itself a totally opposed position to Labour apart from constitutional issues and even more especially Europe. I think that, unless something quite extraordinarily difficult happens in the economy or the government commits some egregious blunders, which of course is never excluded, these will be the most important issues; and of these two I regard Europe as far more acute and capable of arousing major battles than anything else.

On this, of course, the Tory Party has, for the moment, taken a very clear line. I do not know in terms of party political strategy and tactics how valuable that stance of total opposition to our entering the EMU for at least another seven years really is. I find it very difficult to see that it can have an important and continuing attraction for a large enough section of the electorate. However, I believe that perhaps partly for that very reason the Tory Party may possibly go even further than it is now going in the same direction, at least as far as the present leadership is concerned. In other words, I think the opposition to the Single Currency or to EMU, which is still the main point of attack for many in the Tory Party, may increasingly give way to total opposition to the European Union on a very wide front. This is already the case, at least by implication and sometimes even explicitly, for part of the Tory Party. We hear again and again from so-called Euro-sceptics the statement: 'I am not against Europe; I like Europe and I am all in favour of co-operating with Europe. What I am against is our joining the Single Currency and handing over decisions on our economic destiny to Brussels and the bureaucrats of the European Union.' Very often this so-called love for Europe, or at any rate absence of anti-Europeanism, is only skin-deep. It consists of readiness to spend one's holidays on the Costa Brava, on the Riviera or in Tuscany; to enjoy a good meal in a Paris restaurant, maybe even to enjoy some of the performing arts in Continental countries; or, at the most, to be glad if one's children's schools take them on holidays trekking through the Schwarzwald or skiing in the French Alps. But that is about it. This does not really amount to very much and certainly is not a sufficient antidote to opposition to Economic and Monetary Union or at least to adoption of the Single Currency.

Looking ahead, I fear that the Tory Party is quite likely to continue on a much more radical anti-European path than it has adopted even now. Beyond that, if it is to make a real appeal to certain sections of the electorate, it might well adopt a more generally xenophobic stance, the emphasis being on the 'British' way – again, as one might expect, not very clearly defined – but the alternative to the 'third way' is beginning to suggest this tendency. If I am right here, then this xenophobic trend could be very serious for the country, but I do not think it would mean a great deal of advantage for the Tory Party in an electoral clash. It is very difficult to be sure about this. The prospect of Labour being totally European, more particularly totally committed to EMU even long before the election after the end of the first decade, while the Tory Party is radically opposed to it and even shows signs of a xenophobic character, is certainly very disagreeable to contemplate. It may happen, however.

What might change this somewhat sombre outlook is that, as I have said earlier on at one point, the British people are not ready to become really xenophobic or even really anti-European. Large sections of the community, particularly at the moment – and this is not necessarily a 'bull point' – of the financial community and of much of big industry is totally in favour of joining the Single Currency. As I say, this is not necessarily in electoral terms the best thing and could be exploited by an appeal to the instincts of what I suppose one might still call the lower middle class. But at any rate it is a very powerful factor and could in the end persuade the Tory Party, particularly if the present leadership should be diluted, if not replaced, by some of the older leaders who are by no means of the same way of thinking. Then of course we might have a very different situation.

The other point is that if the Tory Party remains stubbornly anti-European, what will be its stance on domestic economic issues? In terms of what has happened elsewhere and the kind of tendencies that one has observed in political swings in other countries, this would open up the possibility of a rather disagreeable type of demagogic appeal to lower-middle-class instincts in terms of welfare, redistributive taxation and all the rest of it. Occasional attacks of political madness can never be ruled out. France, generally speaking a rather rational country in these matters, in recent years has had Boulanger, the Cagoulards and Poujade. Happily there is no Poujade in sight here, but watchfulness is never out of place.

A few words about the Liberal Democrats, leaving aside the complication – as I write – of the announced forthcoming resignation of their leader.

I have to make some assumptions about the situation at the time of the General Election of 2007 and beyond. However fanciful these may be, it is necessary to create a framework without which any speculation of a more specific character becomes impossible. I assume then that Labour has been in power for the preceding five years and enters the election of 2007 having in fact taken the country into the Economic and Monetary Union. I am assuming that its programme will broadly reflect the points I have made above about the party's belief that the country is a middle-class society and that, therefore, the appeal of Labour to the electorate has to be couched in terms that maintain and enlarge the scope of that sort of society. This means that it will reasonably satisfactorily have succeeded in the preceding five years in creating an educational system that is broadly accepted by the population. Similarly, as far as the Health Service is concerned, that it will have found a more rational way of dealing with that and one which, to use the current terminology, is both affordable and provides reasonably adequate service to all sections of the population both in medicine, in surgery and in hospital care or in care at home for the elderly. I also assume that it will have successfully adapted the techniques of our own monetary and fiscal management to the requirements of Economic and Monetary Union and also that Euroland, to which we will then belong, has managed in a reasonably adequate way to create a monetary policy for the whole area, has perhaps even reached some agreements about exchange rate policy with the United States and possibly Japan, and has managed to overcome many internal difficulties that stand in the way of a modest degree of tax harmonization in so far as that is necessary to make a Single Currency and a single monetary policy operate smoothly. I recognize that these are rather optimistic assumptions, but they seem to me to be not unreasonable, subject always to the absence of some major earthquake, political or economic, originating elsewhere.

I am assuming that the Tory Party, having been defeated in the 2002 election, will move heaven and earth to try to regain power in 2007. It may be, and this I think is devoutly to be wished, that its present anti-European stance will have given way, especially when faced with the actual fact of our having adopted the euro and that having worked reasonably well for perhaps three or four years by that time. It may also be that with that will have come a rather more reasonable attitude to many other economic problems, the kind of attitude associated with some of the more moderate, and at the same time more experienced, leaders whom the party has had before 1997 and its defeat in the election.

In that situation what then is the position of the Liberal Democrats and what kind of an image will they offer to the electorate in the election of 2007, which will determine their own fate as well as the broad political landscape for the ensuing decade? The first point on which an assumption has to be made is whether there will have been enough of electoral reform to introduce a substantial, or at least a significant, element of proportional representation into the way we elect our legislators. If this has been the case, and I think it is at least likely, then that would provide the possibility for the Liberal Democrats to obtain a larger representation in parliament and become a more important party to reckon with. But this is only a possibility. To make it a reality would depend on what attractions the Liberal Democrats had to offer the electorate. The comparison would be with Labour, which would enter the election having been in power for a considerable time, and with the Tories, recently revitalized perhaps and refurbished, but still very much opposed to any extension of European integration beyond what has already happened before the election.

As far as Europe is concerned – to the extent that this continues to be a major difference between the two big parties even though from a realistic point of view any continuing Tory opposition may have lost a good deal of its practical relevance – the Liberal Democrats could hardly adopt a significantly different attitude from that of Labour. They have all along been far more united in favouring progress in economic integration, and even though there must be elements in the Liberal Democratic Party and their followers who would be hesitant on wider political union, which may by that time have become something of an issue, nevertheless the party as whole would be unlikely to join any opposition by the Tories to further integration, political or otherwise.

On other matters, constitution for example, one must assume that by 2007 some of the more difficult issues about Scotland, Wales and the government of London will have more or less calmed down and will not be particularly aggressively dealt with by the parties. If the stance of the Labour Party is such as I have assumed, it is not easy to see what exactly the Liberal Democrats could offer that is substantially different. Indeed, if the current attempts to create some degree of co-operation in parliament, even reaching Cabinet committees, between Liberal Democrats and Labour have survived the next seven to eight years and have perhaps even flourished, then one could contemplate some major changes. In fact at that point, however fanciful this may seem, a coalescence between the two parties – in what particular institutional form it is not possible to say – may have taken place. It certainly could lead to electoral alliances, perhaps not over the whole area, but certainly in particular constituencies. At any rate, on the assumption that I have made and allowing for the fact that these are necessarily speculative, it is unlikely in my view that, whatever electoral reform may make possible, the Liberal Democratic Party will suddenly emerge as a major new factor in British politics. I say this despite the fact that as of this moment, given the various discontents that are rife among both Labour supporters and supporters of the Tory Party, as well as among the many remaining 'floating' voters, the Liberal Democrats offer many attractions. These apply particularly to what I may call the intellectual level where the reasoning and reasonable attitude of the Liberal Democrats to many issues of the day, great and small, economic, social, administrative and political, appeal to the good sense and moderate instincts of so many of the electorate. Nevertheless, the Liberal Democrats have not been able to make a real breakthrough and establish themselves as a major factor in politics. I say that for that reason alone it is very unlikely that in the sort of situation that might well exist seven or eight years from now, they could manage things differently.

Speculative though these reflections are, they are still within the conventional framework of party politics that we have known for many decades. Is this right? I think not. In Harold Wilson's reckoning, 'A week is a long time in politics.' If so, eighteen years is an eternity and for that reason alone one cannot be sure that the rules of the game as hitherto played will continue. Also one can never exclude the emergence of some exceptionally visionary politician – or perhaps statesman, one should say – who wishes to depart from the conventional pattern and develop entirely new ideas.

But apart from all this, there is a much more realistic reason, I think, for doubting whether the conventional framework within which I have placed various possibilities of party changes can be preserved. The reason is this. I have already given it as my view that our destiny in the longer term – and that may be even within a couple of decades – will be determined by our place in the world, and more particularly by our place in Europe. In other words, that what happens outside our boundaries will have an increasing influence on how we manage our affairs.

I think Europe is the most important factor in trying to determine how our political life will be lived, say, towards the end of my period under review. There are already substantial movements for enlarging the area of competence and the exercise of power and action by Europe collectively. Quite apart from the battle between the sceptics and those who are in favour of more European integration, there are certain tendencies, particularly in the field of foreign affairs and defence, that seem to push almost inexorably towards united European action. I point only to the events in the Middle East and also to those in Central Europe, particularly in former Yugoslavia. The quite horrendous developments in the latter have led to repeated attempts by Europe either as a whole through the European Union or by more ad hoc arrangements between the most important powers and including some who are not within the European Union, such as Russia, to construct some kind of collective action that would mitigate, and perhaps eventually remove, the continued hostilities and acts of barbarism, as they increasingly are, and produce something resembling peace in the area. In the Middle East too the overwhelming position of the United States as the major outside power – that is to say, outside the parties immediately concerned – to wield influence there has led also to occasional attempts, not particularly successful, by European nations to do so too. As far as Iraq is concerned, of course we have already had one war and warlike developments since that have affected at least one European country, namely our own alongside the United States, but indirectly others, particularly France and Russia.

I think this area of concern, i.e. relations with countries outside Europe and creating some kind of joint defence for the European countries themselves, is bound to push increasingly towards the creation of tighter practices between the European countries and perhaps even to some new and strengthening institutions.

At a first glance, these possible developments in the spheres of defence and foreign affairs appear to raise particularly difficult problems in terms of wider political integration with the possibilities of federal and confederate constitutions raising their heads. They would appear to present such problems for all the members of the European Union, but perhaps more particularly for our own country where the full area of the boundaries of sovereignty that can be preserved has remained a particularly controversial issue, divides all political parties, and will continue to do so, even after we have become members of Euroland.

However, I believe that paradoxically these developments are likely to present fewer problems in this area than one might assume. First of all, many institutions already exist in which collective decisions on foreign policy and defence issues are taken, from the United Nations down to the European Union and the Helsinki organizations, which have to some extent been brought into play in recent difficult situations. Moreover, very often such collective action as seems to be necessary and can in fact be achieved is brought about by ad hoc arrangements without necessarily creating wider institutions where abandonment of national decision-making would become more regular and more permanent. I think, therefore, that much in this area can and will in fact be achieved – I say in fact because circumstances will make it necessary – and will lead to joint action by many of, or all, the members of the European Union, plus many others that are outside the European Union, beyond what might perhaps be expected by looking at the problem in an abstract way.

For these reasons I regard as more important and more difficult what is going to happen on the economic front. Before I consider this I must make certain assumptions of what the situation of this country will be, economically speaking, inside Europe during, say, the second decade that I am dealing with at the moment. I am assuming that some time after the 2002 election we will be members of the European Economic and Monetary Union and will have adopted the Single Currency. It may be that this event will take place even before the election and the referendum, but let us for the moment assume that the present commitment of the government stands. I suppose then that we have passed that hurdle successfully and are members, and that alongside us Denmark and Sweden certainly, possibly Greece also, and perhaps even Norway, which is not as yet a full member of the European Union, may have joined the tighter Economic and Monetary Union, which will then consist of sixteen members. I also assume that even though they have not become members of the Economic and Monetary Union, the countries of Central Europe that have asked for membership – Poland, the Czech Republic, Hungary, perhaps also Romania and Slovenia, and some of the Baltic States, if not all – will have formed some closer association and perhaps become members of the European Union before the year 2017.

Of immediate concern, however, is what is going to be the position of Britain within the sixteen countries, say, which will then form Euroland. It seems to me extremely difficult not to assume that the existence of a Single Currency, of a European Central Bank as well as of a stability pact, which to a large degree constrains the fiscal policy of the member countries, will not inevitably lead to further institutional arrangements. One would be the creation of something almost equivalent to a national Treasury, however that may be constituted, but at any rate a political instance to deal with monetary and economic matters and thus to form a point of reference for the European Central Bank, which is at the moment lacking. And if this were to happen, it seems to me equally impossible to visualize the existence of, as it were, an economic and financial political executive, however formed and with whatever precise powers, that is not also accompanied by the creation of a superimposed body of something like a European Executive of a political character with considerably more powers than the European Commission now has.

I know that this is precisely the point on which Euro-sceptics in the last resort concentrate their attack on our joining the Single Currency. They say that this will inevitably lead to the creation of some kind of federal or confederate political structure, and that this would ultimately of course mean the destruction of our national sovereignty. However, I think that problem will have to be faced, and if the progress of new political institutions in the Union is to be of the kind I have described, it may well need to take place in stages, which could be separated from each other by many years. The first and most immediate would be the creation of an economic and financial authority to correspond to the monetary authority that already exists in the shape of the European Central Bank.

The question will then arise of how that, let alone an even more substantial political authority over a much larger area of what would by then become European rather than national concern, should relate to the legislature – that is to say, what should happen to the European Parliament and whether it can continue in its present form to provide that ultimate democratic element that has been talked about so much.

I believe that inevitably this problem will also have to be tackled and resolved in some form or other. The present skirmishes between the Commission, a sort of embryonic Executive, and the European Parliament, are an indication of the kinds of issue that will have to be faced and resolved in a much more definitive way. But I hesitate to suggest that this would be by the year 2017, though by then it may be clear to some whether they are inevitably on the agenda.

I come back to the reference I made to what was a British proposal, but of which very little, if anything, is heard now, namely to create a bicameral system for the European Union with a Second Chamber composed of members elected from among the national parliaments. This may at the stage that I am now considering offer a very interesting and helpful solution to the problem of the legislative–executive relationship. It would also, of course, ease the progress from the national to the supernational.

At this point I stop and refrain from speculating further on how the relative powers of the Union and of the individual national member states will be distributed. I do not suppose, however, that the national executives and parliaments will disappear. We may find here a process something like the opposite of what might still have to be solved, namely the relations of the Scottish Parliament and the Welsh Assembly to the Westminster Parliament. It would be, as it were, the other way round once you had some kind of supernational structure. How would the remaining national powers be dealt with by what institutions, and to what extent would they remain independent?

In concluding I am bound to say that I realize fully that what I have just said may not only be disputed as a forecast of what might happen, but would furnish considerable ammunition to the opponents of even the next step in European integration, namely our joining the euro. They would point to the fact that they have always argued, and feared, precisely this kind of development.

As I say, this is not anything like a firm forecast of what will happen; it is speculation about certain developments that might occur, and I fully know that these might be quite appalling for some people. I emphasize therefore that my purpose in setting out these developments is not to advocate them but to point to a certain historical dynamic that may bring them about. I think it is not only possible that such developments will take place, but that they will take a variety of forms and be spread over many years. The only thing that I feel confident about is that if the Economic and Monetary Union lasts, which I think it will, it will call for some further developments that some people might describe as of a federal or confederate character and which they would for that reason not like. Nevertheless, I think that they are of a relatively limited character and represent a longer-term evolution, much of which, in terms of greater dependence on the action of others, has already taken place, although it may take far more than the time span I have allowed myself here.

Contrary tendencies have been pointed out by others, described as of a 'tribal' character – that is to say, the urge here and there, far from centralizing certain powers, rather to disperse them more widely. I do not believe that this will be very marked in the more advanced countries of Europe with which I am primarily concerned here, but it cannot be totally ignored.

Finally, there is the question of nationality. I do not believe that nationality is simply a consequence of a collection of powers of government within one particular community. It is not an unimportant feature, but it is certainly not what has produced deep and strong roots of nationhood. There are many other features of a cultural character, first and foremost language, which I think are more important. In this light I do not think that the kind of developments I have described as being ahead of us in the next few decades will damage the sense of national identity of our community.

Index

INDEX

European Monetary System (EMS), 10
European Parliament, 20, 23–5, 69
  clashes with Commission, 24, 170
  powers of, 23
  proposal for bicameral system, 24–5,
    170–1
European Union, 3, 9, 127, 131–2
  Britain's position within, 131–2
  enlargement issue, 25, 33
  future of, 152
  harmonization between different
    countries over issues, 154–6
  and international conflicts, 33
  joint and collective action, 168
  view of inferiority to Britain, 121–2
exchange rates, 84, 122–3
  effect of joining Single Currency, 28
  and monetary policy, 66, 86, 87
executive salaries
  high level of, 64–5
export industries, 84, 122–3, 141

family life, 75
financial services, 40, 68, 120
Financial Services Authority, 68, 93, 120
Financial Services Bill, 120, 127
First World War, 137
fiscal policy, 78, 79–80, 94, 121
  need for combination of monetary
    policy and, 87
France, 32, 140, 163

Gaitskell, Hugh, 43, 54
  consequences of death of, 54
Gang of Four, 61
GATT (General Agreement on Tariffs
  and Trade), 138
Germany, 32
Giscard d'Estaing, 10
globalization, 108
Gold Standard, 137
government
  and intervention in economy, 75, 77–80,
    93–4, 96–7
  supplementation of influence by world
    economy movements, 98
Greece, 32
gross domestic product, 122
Gulf War, 11–12

Hague, William, 161
Haines, Joe, 55

Hattersley, Roy, 57
health service, 8, 48, 71, 159
  in the future, 164
  harmonization between different
    countries, 155–6
  and medical progress, 71, 147
  and nurses, 114–15, 128
  reforms, 62
  separation from welfare, 62–3
  spending on, 117
Home Office, 115
Hong Kong
  incorporation into China, 39
House of Lords
  abolishment of hereditary principle, 61
  reform of, 47, 114, 118, 119–20,
    125–6, 144
  Select Committee on European Affairs,
    120–1
housing, 115

income
  disparity of, 52, 148, 159
  redistribution of taxation to reduce
    differences, 129
income tax, 64
individual
  and authority, 92
Indonesia, 4, 39
inflation, 109
  anti-inflationary policy, 65–6
  and monetary policy, 66, 81–2, 84
  and Stability Pact, 21
  and unemployment, 88
inflation targeting, 85–6, 87, 124
information technology, 74
inheritance tax, 64
interest rates, 81, 122
  control of short-term by Monetary
    Policy Committee, 65–6, 79, 80,
    84, 121, 124
  movements in short-term, 87
  reduction in, 123
  relationship between unemployment
    and movement in, 88
international institutions
  lack of British nationals at head of, 98–9
International Monetary Fund, 4, 44
Iraq, 167
Italy, 32, 105
  abandoning of ERM, 11

175

Japan, 4, 109–12, 113, 131, 132
  decision-making, 111
  economic problems, 4, 38–9
  influence on other economies, 97, 109
  prescription of Keynesian demand
    stimulus, 110
  problems in financial system, 109–10
  social and political structure not attuned
    to requirements of modern
    economy, 110–12
Jenkins, Lord Roy, 10, 61
judiciary, 46, 144–5
justice system, 146
  changes in, 46–7
  harmonization on European Union
    level, 156

Keynes, J. M., 77, 79–80, 88–9, 89–90,
  138, 149

Labour Party
  cooperation with Liberal Democrats,
    61, 166
  disappearance of 'class' image, 58
  media's attitude towards, 14, 58–9
  and trade unions, 6, 8, 58
  see also New Labour government
Labour Party Conference (1998)
  Blair's speech, 103–4
labour policy, 74
Latin America, 139–40
legislation
  and election manifestos, 57, 78
  instrument in changing economy 78, 94
Leontief, Wassily, 73
Liberal Democratic Party, 160, 163, 164–6
  attractions of, 166
  cooperation with Labour Party, 61, 166
  and education, 62
  and electoral reform, 145, 165
  and Europe, 19, 165
  in the future, 164–5
Lincoln, Abraham, 148

M4 (economic indicator), 86
Maastricht Treaty, 21, 151
Macmillan, Harold, 76, 105
macro-economic policy, 65–6, 88, 89,
  141, 149
Major, John, 10, 11–12, 104
  attitude towards Europe by
    administration of, 12

and 'back to basics', 13
difficulties faced by and dissension
  within government of, 9, 12–13
Malaysia, 4, 39
Manifestos, see election manifestos
manufacturing industry, 84, 122, 141
Marquand, David, 57
Marvell, Andrew, 52
media
  attitude towards Labour Party, 14, 58–9
  and Europe, 119
  opposition to joining EMU, 26
medical profession, 154
mergers, 108, 127
Middle East, 142, 167
middle-class society, 128, 158–9, 160
Miners' Union, 8
minimum wage, 116
Minimum Wages Act, 79
Mirror, 59
model-building, 77
monetary policy, 78, 80, 81–90, 91, 94
  and central banks, 21
  debate on execution of, 85–7
  difficult aspects of, 85, 87
  and exchange rates, 66, 86, 87
  handling of by European Central Bank,
    22–3, 28, 31
  and inflation, 66, 81–2, 84
  inflation targeting and monetary
    targeting, 85–7
  and Monetary Policy Committee, see
    Monetary Policy Committee
  need for combination of fiscal policy
    and, 87
  as powerful instrument of economic
    policy, 91
  and unemployment, 81–2, 87–8
Monetary Policy Committee, 22, 88
  determining of short-term interest rates
    by, 65–6, 79, 80, 84, 121, 124
  and inflation, 123–4
  'operationally' independent, 83–4, 91
Monnet, Jean, 138, 152–3
Morrison, Herbert, 53

NAFTA (North American Free Trade
  Area), 34–5, 139
NAIRU (non-accelerating inflation rate of
  unemployment), 88
National Health Service 8, 48; see also
  health service